FAGUS

Annemarie
Jaeggi

FAGUS

Industrial Culture
from Werkbund to Bauhaus

Translated from the German
by Elizabeth M. Schwaiger

Princeton Architectural Press

New York

Published by

Princeton Architectural Press

37 East 7th Street

New York, NY 10003

212.995.9620

For a free catalog of books, call 1.800.722.6657
Visit our website at www.papress.com

Jaeggi, Annemarie: Fagus. Industriekultur zwischen

Werkbund und Bauhaus.

© 1998 by jovis Verlagsbüro

Kurfürstenstraße 15/16

D-10785 Berlin

Project editor: Beth Harrison

Layout: Adam B. Bohannon

Copy editor: Madeline Gutin Perri

Special thanks to: Ann Alter, Eugenia Bell,

Jan Cigliano, Jane Garvie, Caroline Green,

Clare Jacobson, Leslie Ann Kent, Mark Lamster,

Anne Nitschke, Lottchen Shivers, Sara E. Stemen,

Jennifer Thompson, and Deb Wood

of Princeton Architectural Press

—Kevin Lippert, Publisher

This book was made possible by a grant from Inter
Nationes, Bonn.

Front cover: photograph by Albert Renger-Patzsch, April
1928.
Back cover: works photograph, circa 1930.
Frontispiece: driveway and entrance to the Fagus factory,
Photograph by Albert Renger-Patzsch 1928 (Fagus
series No. 1).

ILLUSTRATION CREDITS

Bauhaus Archiv Berlin: pp. 28, 30, 123, 126, 128.
Bauhaus Archiv Berlin, estate of Walter Gropius: pp. 23
   (top), 33, 35 (right), 40, 51, 53, 56, 114.
Bauhaus Archiv Berlin, estate of Adolf Meyer: pp. 2, 37,
   108, 116.
Bauhaus Archiv Berlin, Markus Hawlik Photography: pp.
   16, 17, 20, 24, 36, 37, 69, 71-74, 79, 80, 82-87, 125
   (top), 127, 130.
Bauhaus Archiv Berlin, Gunter Lepkowski Photography: p.
   101.
Courtesy of the Busch-Reisinger Museum, Harvard Univer-
   sity Art Museums, Gift of Walter Gropius, © President
   and Fellows of Harvard College, Harvard University: p.
   34, bottom.
Der Baumeister 37.1939, advertising leaflet (private collec-
   tion): p. 59 (bottom).
Archives Foto Marburg: 9. 23.
Denkmalpflege in Baden-Württemberg (Conservation in Baden
   Wurttemberg) 21. 1992, issue 3, p. 13: p. 59 (top).
Engineering News 53.1905, No. 21, p. 543: p. 58.
Fagus Factory, Alfeld/Leine, Karl Schünemann Photogra-
   phy: p. 125 (bottom), 132.
Robert Grimshaw: Die kaufmännische Propaganda (Commer-
   cial Propaganda). (Dresden 1913), p. 21: p. 41.
Der Industriebau 4.1913, issue I: pp. 15 (bottom), 25, 27, 31
   (bottom), 32 (bottom).
Götz & Ilsemann, Engineers, Hildesheim: pp. 134, 136-37.
Jahrbuch des Deutschen Werkbundes (Deutscher Werkbund
   Yearbook) 2.1913, fig. 1: p. 42.
Johannes-Molzahn-Centrum, Kassel: p. 98 (right).
Kunst und Künstler (Art and Artists) 27.1928/29, issue 8, p.
   309: p. 54.
Karl Scheffler: Die Architektur der Großstadt (Urban Archi-
   tecture). (Berlin 1913), p. 162: p. 43.
Evert van Straaten (Ed.): Theo van Doesburg 1883-1931.
   (s'Gravenhage 1983), p. 138: p. 102.
Helmut Weber: Gropius und das Faguswerk (Munich 1961):
   p. 29, 72.
Fagus archives, Ernst und Gerd Greten, permanent loan to
   Bauhaus archives Berlin: all other illustrations.

Library of Congress Cataloging-in-Publication Data
Jaeggi, Annemarie.
[Fagus. English]
Fagus : industrial culture from Werkbund to Bauhaus / Annemarie Jaeggi; [translated by Elizabeth M. Schwaiger].
   p. cm.
Includes bibliographical references.
1-56898-175-9 (alk. paper)
1. Fagus-Werk (Alfeld, Lower Saxony, Germany) 2. Shoe industry—Germany—History.
3. Leather industry and trade—Germany—History. 4. Architecture, Industrial—Germany—Case studies. I. Title.
HD9787.A4-Z.G(Germany).x4A-Z.F(Fagus)
338.7'685'0943—dc21   99-053589

Contents

Introduction

Who hasn't heard of the Fagus factory in Alfeld an der Leine? The factory, designed by a young Walter Gropius and Adolf Meyer and in construction from 1911 onward, is generally taken to be the seminal building of the modern movement in architecture. It is featured in all dictionaries of architecture. Imprinted on our consciousness like no other building, the Fagus factory embodies the revolution that took place in twentieth-century architecture.

In the case of the Fagus factory, the client and his architects were unusually well matched. Carl Benscheidt Sr. was a manufacturer who combined a progressive entrepreneurial spirit with the philosophy of the social reform movement of the time. He produced shoe lasts, implementing highly improved production methods in combination with the latest discoveries in orthopedic research. Quality and innovation were his maxims. In a complete departure from established norms, the architects succeeded in providing the extraordinary company with an unusual image; combining the utilitarian character of the factory as a functional building with a generous use of glass, they achieved a new form of representation. The building became part of an advertising strategy that emphasized the distinctive novelty of its product.

The AEG in Berlin served as Benscheidt's model. From 1907 onward, the AEG's artistic advisor, Peter Behrens, worked toward creating a corporate identity with a consistent artistic vision that reached from the architecture to the products and down to the publications and brochures. The Fagus factory was to receive the same identity-building treatment. However, in the case of Fagus, the concept would not be in the hands of a single artist; instead, it would involve many different experts.

Gropius and Meyer assembled the group with a sure hand. Only the best were chosen: Max Hertwig, Johannes Molzahn, Theo van Doesburg, and Herbert Bayer submitted ideas for the corporate image; with a series of photographs, Albert Renger-Patzsch produced what has become the definitive portrait of the Fagus factory and its products; the Bauhaus workshops were charged with designing the interior and the office furniture. The choice to involve primarily young artists focused on innovation was unusual in the 1920s. No other enterprise in the Germany of the Weimar Republic had such close ties to the avant-garde.

The AEG and Fagus were not alone in formulating such broad visions during the years preceding the First World War. Rather, they belonged to a group of enlightened companies that helped the modern movement to succeed. These predominantly young companies introduced new consumer products to the market by means of effective advertising. Under the umbrella of the Deutscher Werkbund (DWB)—an association of entrepreneurs, scientists, artists, and writers, founded in 1907—their goal was to promote Germany's position in the global market through high standards in product quality and design.

Raising product quality and improving product design were linked to an educational agenda: to elevate consumer taste and to awaken a greater awareness of beauty. Style and dignity, it was felt, are transferable from product to consumer—the product was both a material and a spiritual possession. Indeed, to the Deutscher Werkbund, industry and trade now conveyed culture instead of state and church, which had previously performed this role, and this change brought with it a true paradigm shift.

When applied to factory architecture, this philosophy translated into a new approach to valuation. Previously located between the poles of plain utilitarianism and ostentatious advertising, the factory was now elevated to a "cathedral of work." Within this broader context, companies drew their identity from the architecture—through the impact of its external image and its community-building contribution among the workers. The progressive manufacturer realized that a dark workplace and poor working conditions led not only to dissatisfaction but also to poor performance and, hence, inferior products.

Fagus was a company that was well aware of these relationships. Model interiors, higher wages, and social benefits served the good of the labor force; more importantly, they also guaranteed harmony, efficiency, and productivity at the workplace. In the paternalistic Fagus company, everyone was supposed to feel like a member of a larger family, where trust was mutual and reciprocal. Hence, there were no work or labor contracts.

The work of Gropius and Meyer must be seen in the context of this encompassing concept of industrial culture. For a period of fifteen years, they oversaw not only the architecture but all details pertaining to the building: interior design, furniture, lighting fixtures, and fittings; even foot mats and wire fencing, originated in their design studio. In addition, they worked on a variety of private commissions for the manufacturer, from tombstone to villa. The Fagus factory was a unique expression of both Bauhaus ideals: the *Gesamtkunstwerk* of the "great building," formulated in the founding manifesto of 1919, and the motto that followed after 1923: "Art and Technology—a New Unity."

Artists were also consulted on technical and organizational matters at Fagus. Thus Gropius and Meyer, as well as Molzahn, presented design sketches for an apparatus developed by Karl Benscheidt Jr. for the shoe-producing industry. Even while he was constructing a Fagus precision lathe, the most accurate duplicating machine of the 1920s worldwide, the junior works manager strove to bring functionality, safety, and form into harmony. Production tools should not only function well, they should also be safe and beautiful—a concept meant to satisfy both the buyer and the operator on all levels: technology, health, and aesthetics.

Following reformist philosophy, the ultimate goal of father and son Benscheidt was to elevate the level of public health. They produced lasts to counteract the deformation and discomfort caused by poorly constructed footwear; their lasts were formed to create naturally fitting shoes. To this end, they generously supported orthopedic research and were founding members, around 1926, of a company that would translate theory into practice: the production of anatomically correct but nevertheless fashionable shoes. The concept was introduced to the market with an enormous advertising campaign, with graphic design by Molzahn and requisite photography by Renger-Patzsch.

When the worldwide economic crisis hit in 1929, Fagus could no longer afford to collaborate with artists. Few companies in this sector survived the following years, but Fagus was among those that did. Its survival was founded in constant innovation of manufacturing tools with patented inventions, and quick reactions to changes in the market. The archives offer no answer to the question of whether or not the concept of corporate identity turned out to be financially viable. Whatever the outcome of a closer study of this question might be, in terms of cultural history, this is one of the most remarkable experiments of the modern movement and, in the context of the history of architecture, it marks the beginning of a new era.

Until now, the critical literature on the Fagus factory has focused on its architecture and on Walter Gropius, concentrating mainly on the trendsetting main building. This book, however, emphasizes the idea of industrial culture; architecture, interior design, graphic design, and photography are placed in the context of the business philosophy and the advertising strategy of a company. The narrative begins with the founding of the factory in 1911 and ends with the last collaboration between factory and artists in the late 1920s.

The principal source and basis for this book were the archives of the Fagus factory. Although little material has survived about the early years prior to the First World War, the archives on the whole overwhelm with an abundance of material that enables us to look at the topic from a fresh perspective: three hundred folders of correspondence, approximately five hundred plans (mostly blueprints of drawings from Gropius's studio), some two hundred vintage prints from professional photographers, and countless glass-plate negatives bear witness in unprecedented scope and quality to an industrial culture in the modern movement.

It is no easy task to choose wisely from such a selection. Naturally, architecture plays a leading role. When we consider that the estates of Gropius and Meyer contain only a single drawing of the Fagus factory, then it becomes clear what an immense source of information the archives present on this issue alone.

In some instances, familiar and existing information is stated anew. This applies, above all, to historic dates and facts. But even here, new aspects arise: we came to realize that our evaluation of the Fagus factory was by no means shared by contemporaries in the beginning of the century, nor does our view reflect Gropius's own at the time. Ours is grounded in a retrospective interpretation put forward in the late 1920s, essentially by Gropius himself.

The perception of the Fagus factory as a modern exponent—as it were, as an example of the International Style—owes much to the masterful photography of Albert Renger-Patzsch. His series on the Fagus factory, created in 1928, captures the architecture as well as the products. Few of these images have ever been published before and the extensive series is presented here for the first time in its specific context.

These photographs, however, have also perpetuated the myth that an innovative method of construction was required for the glazing in the main building of the Fagus factory. This is a gross misapprehension. To clarify the issue, expert Jürgen Götz has contributed a chapter on the Fagus factory from the perspective of structural engineering. Since 1982, Götz has been in charge of maintaining and renovating the Fagus buildings, which gives him a unique familiarity with the fabric of these structures. In his contribution, he discusses the construction, the structural damage, and the necessary repairs at Fagus.

Like all authors, I owe thanks to many individuals. First and foremost are Ernst Greten and Gerd Greten, who gave me access to the Fagus archives. Their trust in me, and the unlimited freedom I was granted during my six-week stay at the Fagus factory, enabled me to begin processing the immense volume of material. Franziska Greten gave me support in important matters of organization and was my intrepid guide into even the darkest basement rooms.

All the material from the Fagus factory archives has been given as a permanent loan to the Bauhaus archives in Berlin, where I was received in the most welcoming manner. My thanks are due to its director, Dr. Peter Hahn, for a renewed and, once again, fruitful collaboration. I feel especially indebted to Dr. Christian Wolsdorff, curator and head of the architectural department at the Bauhaus archives. His careful reading of the manuscript and his far-reaching knowledge enriched this book. Furthermore, Dr. Wolsdorff handled not only the cataloging of the visual material but also served as editor.

Jutta Jahn, née Benscheidt, was always willing to answer my seemingly never-ending questions with patience and unfailing interest in my work. I have profited immensely from her lively reminiscences and the privilege of viewing personal documents.

Jürgen Götz opened my eyes to the architecture of the Fagus factory in many respects. His dedication and cooperation helped see the project through to completion. Finally, my sincere thanks go to the staff of the Fagus factory. As representatives of the entire team, I would like to name Inge Naumann, Karl Schünemann, and Kurt Vesterling.

Several institutions and individuals have generously supported my work and for this I would like to express my sincere gratitude: Ute Brüning, Berlin; Stephanie Ehret (Klingspor Museum, Offenbach); Sybille Eckenfels, Karlsruhe; Sjarel Ex (Centraal Museum, Utrecht); Galerie Ulrich Fiedler, Cologne; Virginia Heckert, New York; Dr. Renate Heidt-Heller (Wilhelm Lehmbruck Museum, Duisburg); Burkhard Jahn, Alfeld; Helmut Knocke (City Archives of Hanover); Klaus Lill, Hanover; Dr. Rauschmann, (German Society for Orthopaedics and Traumatology, Orthopaedic Historic Research, Frankfurt/Main); Hans-Peter Reisse (Johannes Molzahn Centrum, Kassel); Renate Scheper, Berlin; Dr. Rolf Stümpel (Deutsches Technik Museum, Berlin); Dr. Klaus-Dieter Thomann, Frankfurt/Main; Prof. Dr. Helmut Weber, Hanover; Ann and Jürgen Wilde (Albert Renger-Patzsch Archives, Cologne).

I would also like to extend my gratitude to the colleagues and members at the Institute of Art History of the University of Karlsruhe. Without their understanding and tolerance, this book would never have come into being. Most of all, I would like to thank the late Prof. Dr. Johannes Langner, Freiburg/Br., who accompanied the progress of this book with encouraging interest and well-intentioned criticism.

A.J.

Modern Entrepreneurship

The Manufacturer

When Carl Benscheidt (1858–1947) founded the Fagus factory in 1911, he was already a man of fifty-three with an active and successful life behind him. At an age when others begin to contemplate retirement, he launched a new enterprise, although he could have chosen to settle into a financially secure existence. It was Benscheidt's dedication to work, his pronounced social conscience, and his pursuit of a healthy lifestyle—characteristics and interests rooted in his origins and early years—that enabled him to take such a daring step.

The oldest of twelve children, Carl Benscheidt grew up in the Sauerland region of Germany. Chronic illness prevented him from taking over the family farm and a lack of financial means precluded a higher education. His health improved as he began to follow a naturopathic diet and lifestyle; from the age of seventeen, Benscheidt was a vegetarian, never smoked, and drank alcohol only in moderation. Right through to old age, he took early-morning barefoot walks across dew-covered meadows. As well, he tried to strengthen himself and improve his fitness through hard physical labor.

As Carl Benscheidt's greatest desire—to study medicine—remained out of reach, he worked from 1877 to 1879 in the naturopathic centers of Arnold Rikli in Veldes (Bled) and Trieste.[1] Rikli investigated why many of his patients had foot complaints and concluded that these were caused by shoes that did not fit the anatomy of the human foot. Prototype lasts, requested by Rikli from Switzerland, were used to produce foot-friendly shoes, with great therapeutic success. One of Benscheidt's tasks was to measure patients for fitted lasts. When he returned to

Carl Benscheidt Sr. Photo by Albert Renger-Patzsch, April 1928. Fagus series no. 54.

Opposite: Fagus lasts. Factory photo, circa 1930.

Late nineteenth century. Symmetric shoe last with wood block and leather cover. Factory photo, circa 1930.

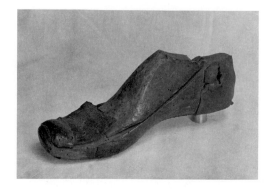

Germany, his connection to the Lebensreformbewegung (a German social reform movement of the late nineteenth century) brought him into contact with the co-op fruit farm "Eden" in Oranienburg near Berlin. He observed discord and tension among the planters, however, and this deterred him from joining the new colony.

Benscheidt began to carve lasts for friends and acquaintances, but very few shoemakers were willing to use the foot-friendly lasts because they made the shoemaker's work more labor intensive. The established procedure of the time was to manufacture shoes based on symmetric lasts with no difference to accommodate the left and right foot. While this made things easier for the shoemaker, the shoes had to be broken in, to the detriment of the wearer's feet. Benscheidt decided to found his own workshop in 1884 in Hanover, where he produced both lasts and shoes.

Even at this early stage, he was adept at drawing attention to himself through clever advertising. Benscheidt practiced a type of campaign known as self-advertising. He would write to a local newspaper under a false name, complaining about the lack of quality footwear. In the next issue, Benscheidt would then draw attention to his own workshop. "This ad was repeated several times under different guises. It cost next to nothing and was very effective."[2] Benscheidt may have been emulating advertising strategies practiced by the naturopaths, an assumption supported by the fact that he published his expert knowledge in newspapers and brochures.[3]

These efforts brought Benscheidt to the attention of shoe-last manufacturer Carl Behrens, whose factory was located in Alfeld an der Leine near Hanover. In 1887, Carl Behrens hired Benscheidt as works manager. The factory specialized in the production of form-fitted lasts, which shoemakers bought from sales representatives. Usually, shoemakers would carve their own lasts out of wood, but for fashionable shoes, they needed up-to-date fitted lasts. From the late 1850s onward, these were machine-produced on lathes.

The demand for lasts for the manufacture of shoes was still relatively low in Germany at that time because the quality of factory-made shoes could not compete with that of handmade shoes. This situation changed drastically in 1891, when the American company Goodyear introduced the welt stitcher. Suddenly, lasts were in high demand. Benscheidt was quick to recognize this trend and made contact with the Americans, who had already begun to establish shoe factories in Europe in order to market their machines. He negotiated a contract stipulating that each would recommend the other's products—namely, lasts and stitching machines. This coup translated into a rapid boost in business for Behrens, who quickly became the leading shoe-last manufacturer in Germany.

Wooden last turning lathe, circa 1870. Factory photo circa 1930.

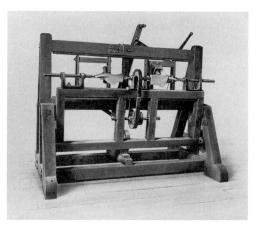

Shoe-last factory. C. Behrens. Architect: Eduard Werner. Photo by Karl F. Wunder, circa 1898.

The mass production that now ensued called not only for greater precision in shoe lasts but also for exact tools, customized to the new manufacturing process. For each model and for each standard shoe size, the shoe manufacturer required the matching clicking knife to cut the soles and the upper leather. Under Benscheidt's management, Behrens became the first shoe-last manufacturer to establish an in-house forge and to develop the technical know-how required to produce these tools. And, finally, the punching-out of leather pieces called for tough counters; hence, Behrens introduced cutting blocks and clicking tables into its product line. This array of specialized products enabled the manufacturer to provide the best service to the shoe industry and gave it a clear advantage over its competitors.

When Carl Behrens died in 1896, Carl Benscheidt became general manager, together with businessman Wilhelm Bertram. In 1897, he oversaw the building of a new factory, which had become necessary due to the company's growth. Designed by Eduard Werner, an architect from Hanover, the new building was an innovative complex equipped with state-of-the-art American shoe-last lathes and an optimized dust-extraction system. Transmission and ducts were accommodated in the basement, an American solution that was new to Germany.[4] Another feature that attracted a lot of attention was the system of conveyor belts used for waste removal in the sawmill. One critic stated that "light, cleanliness, and organization" in the factory halls "have a moral effect on the work ethic, which is of no small import for the profitability of the works."[5]

Indeed, Benscheidt attached great importance to the educational value of a building and its interior layout and furnishings. After years of dispute with the labor force, he succeeded in establishing discipline based on patriarchal severity and improved conditions. Benscheidt introduced fixed work hours and a regular payment schedule; he was strongly opposed to alcohol consumption at the workplace, common at the time. His concern for the workers' well-being became manifest in the facilities of the new building—for example, the dining

Shoe-last factory. C. Behrens. Production hall. Photo by Karl F. Wunder, circa 1898.

hall, the changing room with lockers, showers, and tub baths.

Benscheidt also developed a remarkable social conscience with regard to workers' housing. In 1899 he was a founding member of the Gemeinnütziger Bauverein Alfeld (Alfeld Building Cooperative) and persuaded five other manufacturers to contribute to the initial investment. The municipality of Alfeld was, however, less keen and refused to sell off land for the development. The cooperative therefore purchased land from a farmer on the edge of Gerzen, a neighboring community, and established the Kolonie Buchenbrink. The settlement consisted of typified detached houses with gardens. Architect Eduard Werner designed the plans. Another settlement, Am Rodenkamp, followed a few years later, this time in Alfeld.

On the one hand, Benscheidt's paternalistic care sprang from his own humble background. On the other hand, as a farsighted and clever businessman, he recognized that worker and manufacturer depend on one another. The factory is profitable when the workers are working well. To this end, well-trained, motivated, and loyal personnel are essential. Benscheidt always looked on his workers as living capital that should be cared for. In turn, each worker who adhered to Benscheidt's rules would benefit from having a guaranteed workplace and social benefits, which were unusual for the time.

The Foundation

After twenty years of work at Behrens, irreconcilable differences with the heirs prompted Benscheidt to resign on October 2, 1910. A few months before that, Carl Behrens Jr. had

Buchenbrink colony. Architect: Eduard Werner, begun in 1901.

challenged, "Why don't you go into competition with us? But you're too much of a coward!"[6] Deeply hurt, Benscheidt prepared to create his own company while still at Behrens. From the start, he knew that success was possible only if he "could surpass Behrens on all levels."[7]

From his son-in-law, Ludwig Menge, Benscheidt secured an option to buy the Neue Wiese (New Meadow), a three-hectare building site directly opposite Behrens's factory with a private rail spur that linked the property to the nearby Hanover-Göttingen line. To finance his purchase, Benscheidt began negotiating from June 1910 onward with the United Shoe Machinery Corporation in Beverly, Massachusetts, near Boston. The corporation, which had merged with Goodyear, planned to establish a direct source of last production for its shoe factories in Germany and saw in Benscheidt the ideal partner for such a joint venture.

On October 10, 1910—a mere week after his resignation—Carl Benscheidt left Alfeld to travel to the United States in the company of his eldest son Karl Benscheidt Jr. (1888–1975). In Boston, the partners were impressed with their long-term business associate from Germany as a self-made man and soon signed an agreement with him; the United Shoe Machinery Corporation assumed 80 percent of the total estimated cost of one million marks. Benscheidt Sr., appointed as sole and permanent directing manager, was responsible for the remainder. In return, he agreed to purchase the machinery required for last production from his American venture partner.

When Benscheidt Sr. returned to Germany in November 1910, his son stayed behind for an entire year. There he worked in different factories, among others in the clicking-knife department of the United Shoe Machinery Corporation in Beverly, to learn as much as he could about the latest developments in shoe production. The young graduate from Berlin's business management school was also interested in studying the efficient American approach to management. When the Fagus factory opened, he returned to Alfeld, and his first task was to train the workers on the new machines. His range of responsibilities in the paternal factory included technical know-how, works management, and advertising. In addition, Benscheidt Jr. began his own intensive research in orthopedics.

On his return to Alfeld on November 20, 1910, Carl Benscheidt Sr. immediately began to organize the purchase of the lumber necessary for last production. Because untreated wood had to be well seasoned prior to further processing, he decided to set up a temporary sawmill. All preparations for starting up the new factory were similarly undertaken in the shortest possible time. The name of the new company, on the other hand, was discussed at length with the American partners; conventional names such as Eagle, Anchor, and Achilles were among the suggestions, as was Lastco.[8] The company was officially founded on March 28, 1911, as Fagus GmbH, after the Latin name for the beech tree, its wood being the most important raw material in shoe-last production.

In contrast to C. Behrens Alfelder Schuhleisten-Fabriken, Benscheidt used neither his own name nor the location in the company name. On the contrary, with Fagus he had chosen a short and memorable word whose Latin etymology gave it an air of reliability, even of science. While Behrens had chosen a beech leaf as his logo—the brand was known in England and the United States as the Leaf Brand[9]—Benscheidt was happy to go to the heart of the matter and name the object for what it was. He very quickly registered the word *Fagus* as a trademark, first in Germany and then across Europe, including Russia.

Trademarks for C. Behrens and Fagus.

The main reason for Benscheidt's decision to found his factory in Alfeld was a readily available workforce already trained in last manufacture and in producing clicking knives, and he therefore rejected more advantageous land offers from other communities. Benscheidt began by recruiting individual workers away from Behrens, and soon there was a wave of defections. At the beginning of 1912, with the Fagus factory nearly completed, he already employed 150 workers who had defected from Behrens and was able to start production without delay.

The breadth of these considerations has been summarized by Benscheidt as follows: "I was at the time so well known in the industry that my career and the development of the new factory became the subject of daily discussions and speculation. . . . My products were exemplary because of the trained workers and good facilities, and my achievements attracted a lot of attention. Almost overnight I was seen as the manufacturer who had surpassed Behrens."[10]

The Factory: Grounds and Layout

Once again, Carl Benscheidt approached architect Eduard Werner (1847–1923), this time to create plans for the Fagus factory. He could hardly have found a more experienced architect for building a shoe-last factory: Werner had not only designed the new building for Behrens in 1897 but had also been in charge of all subsequent expansions. Moreover,

Factory grounds of Fagus and C. Behrens, 1911.

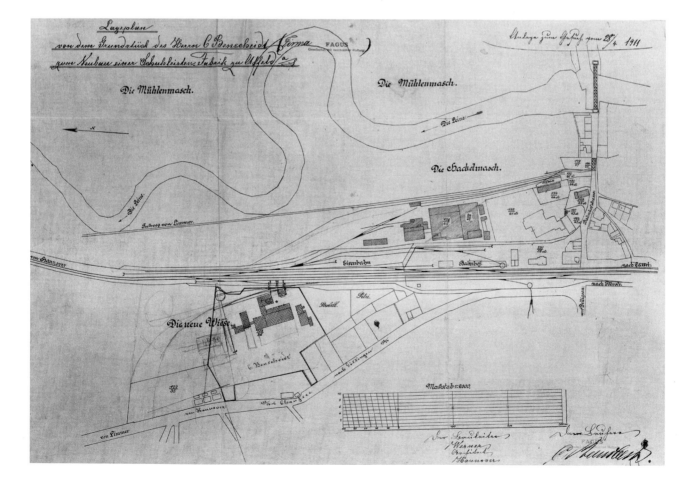

the architect still had all the materials of that project at hand, from drawings to invoices—a great help in facilitating not only the project planning but also the cost calculation.[11]

It appears that at the beginning of his career Werner had worked for Wallbrecht, a building contractor and real-estate speculator in Hanover. In 1886, he made the jump into self-employment and specialized in industrial construction and workers' housing.[12] Among other projects, he had built the ironworks in Wülfel and the factory hall for a mattress manufacturer in Hanover-Linden (1913).[13] He was commissioned by the Körting company to build the Colonie Körtingsdorf in Hanover-Badenstedt (1889–1891) and also the workers' housing development for the Portland cement factory Vorwohle.[14]

Carl Benscheidt appreciated the solid execution and functionality of Werner's architecture. As he stated in his memoirs, "Werner always built according to the same model, with the advantage that he was able to accurately project cost and labor and that his drawings, calculations, and estimates were 100 percent reliable."[15] After his return from the United States, Benscheidt contacted Werner immediately and they began to formulate a plan for the "ideal factory layout"[16] on a scale that was approximately one-quarter of Behrens's establishment.

The 1897 construction for Behrens's shoe-last factory was the model for the new factory in almost every way. The Fagus factory too was designed with the production processes in mind, to avoid superfluous transportation paths and unnecessary detours. In the interest of optimized operation, Benscheidt eliminated all the elements he judged as faulty. The Fagus factory, for example, had only one elevator, while Behrens's required five because of its lay-

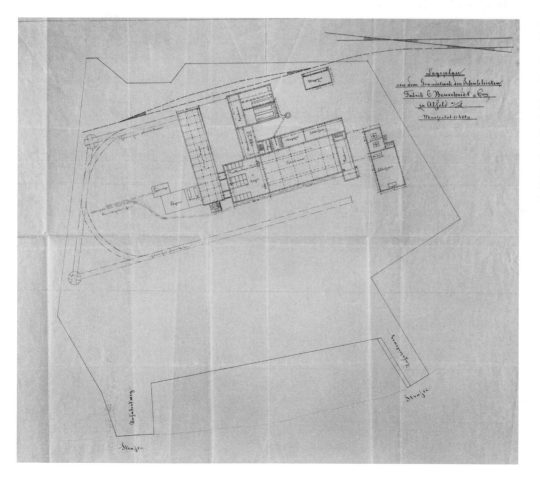

Ground plan of complex. Planning status in February 1911. Design: Eduard Werner. Functional axis from left to right: Sawmill with steam chambers, warehouse, drying kilns, production hall, main building. Separately: clicking-knife department. On railway side: boiler house and power house, woodshaving and coal storage, warehouse.

out. This modification alone not only shortened paths and saved time, but it also reduced the number of workers required to operate and maintain the equipment.

The major drawback of the Behrens factory lay in the unfortunate shape of its lot, which was long and narrow. In 1897, during the planning phase of the new building, Benscheidt had pointed out the difficulties connected with any future expansion of the complex, trying in vain to convince the Behrens family that the lot on the other side of the train tracks, the so-called New Meadow, offered much better possibilities. Now Benscheidt was building the Fagus factory on that very lot. From the beginning, the natural expansion that would go hand in hand with improving production techniques was taken into consideration; all future expansions were to be simple additions to the existing fabric.[17]

The Fagus factory ran parallel to a private rail spur. The northwest-southeast functional axis was bordered by the sawmill with boiler house, the warehouse and drying kilns, the production hall, and the main building with shipping and handling facilities. This layout corresponded to the main steps in the production of a shoe last: the beech logs were split into wedge-shaped blocks in the sawmill and then shaped into rough lasts on the so-called roughing lathes. Next, the rough lasts were transported to large steam boilers, where they remained for several hours before being stacked in the warehouse—a huge building, well ventilated but completely sealed off against incoming light. Here the rough lasts were left to dry for several years. This was followed by an artificial drying process until the wood reached a maximum residual humidity of 7 to 8 percent. Finally, the rough lasts were taken to the production hall, where the lathes stood. With the help of a copying lathe, the shape of a handmade last model was transferred to the rough last. During that process, different sizes could be made by proportional adjustments. This was followed by various sanding and polishing processes, then several quality-control steps, until the finished last was ready for packaging and shipping.

A boiler and machine house, as well as separate storage bunkers for wood shavings and coal, was located next to the main complex on the railroad side. The coal required to operate the steam boiler was unloaded right in front of the building and the wood shavings—a profitable waste product—were automatically sorted into grades and gathered for removal. The clicking-knife department (forge and tool-and-die shop) was clearly set

Creating a shoe last: beech logs in the factory yard; splitting the logs into wedges; rough lasts drying in the warehouse; forming on the lathe; quality control. Photos by Albert Renger-Patzsch, April 1928. Fagus series no. 27, 29, unnumbered, 31, 38.

apart from the last production section in the southeast area of the complex. Horse-drawn wagons—later, trucks—for delivery and transport entered and exited through the gate that opened onto adjacent Hannoversche Strasse.

Although the Fagus factory complex was a great improvement over Behrens's with regard to operation and technology, its layout was basically the same, even in terms of orientation. On both sites, the three-story main building faced Alfeld, its height shielding the lower shed building of the production hall. Benscheidt, however, knew how to make the most of the main building facing the tracks. In contrast to Behrens, who obviously viewed the railway merely as a means of transportation, the founder of Fagus understood that the facade overlooking the train tracks could be an effective platform for advertising.

In Eduard Werner's plan, the overall shape of the complex appeared as a row of buildings with different functions. With the exception of the main building, which contained the production rooms and offices, the buildings were plain and utilitarian, conforming to average aesthetic requirements. In keeping with the time, brick was selected as the main building material; only the five-story warehouse was to be a half-timbered construction.

The single-story shed building of the production hall was designed on a rectangular grid whose component units were 7 meters x 5 meters. Cast-iron columns placed at the intersecting points support the wooden roof structure. The three-story main building surrounded the production hall on two sides; the latter projecting into the ground floor of the wing that faced the railroad. Eduard Werner's logical solution was to apply the same grid to the main building and to integrate it into the facade design, bringing order to the overall structure.

He divided the main facades with multistory piers that match the grid and are spaced at 5–meter intervals on the railroad side. Two slender lesenes, reminiscent of Gothic mullions, articulate the bays and connect with segmented lintels on the third floor. By contrast, Werner divided the 7–meter intervals of the southeast side with 3.5–meter-wide bays, adding a row of pointed blind arches as a balustrade for the large windows. The corner section, built on a square ground plan, created a visual link between the two facades; in this section, they seemed to merge. Coherence was provided by the band of segmented arch windows on the third floor.

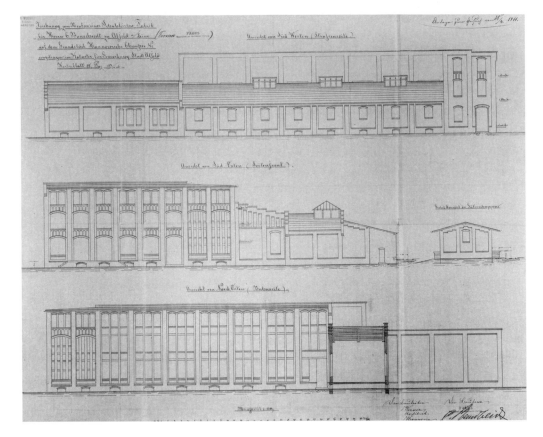

The more elaborate design and the large windows marked this flat-roofed building as the main structure of the complex. At the same time, the different facades corresponded to the varied usage and light conditions. In this manner, the packaging department was located behind the large openings on the ground floor of the southeast wing; two of the windows were, in fact, large, projecting loading platforms, while a third provided access to the main staircase. On the other hand, Werner maintained the wide bays on the northeast side to allow for the maximum of natural light. It is interesting to note that the different uses of ground floor and upper level, production hall, offices, and executive suite, respectively, were not reflected in the design treatment. Only the corner section, where the washroom facilities and wardrobe were located, was clearly different in design by way of small windows.

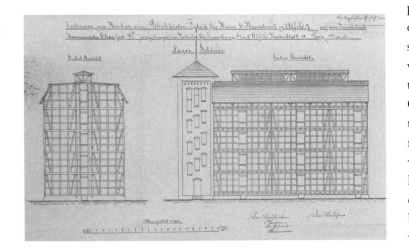

On the railroad side, the main building connected to the saddleback-roofed machine house and, at a right angle, with a single-story complex consisting of boiler house, coal storage, and wood-shaving bunker. This grouping formed a long, low slab that left no opening for access between the main building and the railroad track. Next to it stood the detached single-story warehouse.

Werner's design was submitted to the municipal authorities in April 1911 and building permission was granted in May. However, the Berlin architects Walter Gropius and Adolf Meyer had already been commissioned to redesign the facades of the entire factory complex. Carl Benscheidt Sr.'s dissatisfaction with Werner's work in this regard had already become evident. Three years earlier, in 1908, the Alfeld Building Association had commissioned another architect known for his work in the neo-Biedermeier style fashionable at the time. Werner was a member of the Hanover School, characterized by the use of spare brick decor as a throwback to Gothicism, stepped gables, and segmental arched windows. At sixty-three, he represented the old generation, and Benscheidt's visit to the United States must have opened his eyes as to how outdated Werner's industrial architecture had become.

Aesthetics aside, this collaboration with Werner resulted in one of the most modern installations, considered exemplary not only for its time but for many decades to come.[18] In the Fagus factory, Benscheidt created a customized factory, an ideal complex precisely because he brought all his experience as works manager to the project. In a presentation in 1927, Karl Benscheidt Jr. drew attention to this aspect: "Just think of the implications when one man undertakes to build a large factory twice during his lifetime, having access— in both instances—to sufficient means to implement the ideas he had recognized as correct and essential."[19]

The Factory: Exterior Design

From the United States, Carl Benscheidt Sr. wrote to a friend in Alfeld with news of the successful negotiations and the imminent construction of the Fagus factory. The friend passed on this exciting news to the local press and, upon his return, Benscheidt was deluged with offers. Among them was a bid dated December 7, 1910, from architect Walter Gropius, whose brother-in-law, Max Burchard (Alfeld's district magistrate) had informed him of Benscheidt's building plans.[20] To add weight to the bid, Max Burchard seems to have contacted Carl Benscheidt personally.[21]

On January 12, 1911, Gropius received written confirmation of Benscheidt's interest, with the proviso, however, that a known and reliable local architect—meaning Eduard Werner, of course—would be in charge of the project as a whole and also of "the interior layout and outfitting of the buildings. . . . However, I feel quite differently about the exterior design of the buildings. In this aspect, the aforementioned gentleman may not be able to meet my expectations and insofar as you are willing to participate in the project in this manner, I would gladly avail myself of your services."[22]

The main reason for Benscheidt's interest in Gropius lay in the latter's previous work with architect Peter Behrens. In his covering letter, Gropius had mentioned not only this collaboration but had given proof of his expertise by referring to the factory buildings for the Allgemeine Elektrizitäts Gesellschaft (AEG; General Electric Corporation). With these buildings in Berlin, Behrens had set new standards in architecture, elevating the task of building factories to art. Benscheidt Sr. was aware of Behrens's work from the publication *Der Industriebau* and expressed the "wish to create something of comparable quality, and moreover, as my new factory complex will lie on the heavily traveled Hamburg-Frankfurt route, an exemplary building could also be an excellent advertisement."[23]

Gropius replied to Benscheidt Sr. "that, as a member of the Deutscher Werkbund, whose aim it is to promote a true collaboration between industry and art, I would do everything to utilize the excellent resources of this organization to the advantage of your building."[24] Gropius would indeed seize every occasion to publicize the Fagus factory, as a prime example of modern architecture, with exhibitions and publications of the Werkbund, to which he had only just been voted a member in December 1910.

The Fagus project rescued Gropius from a difficult situation. He was just setting out in his profession and was constantly short of funds, as contracts were scarce in the new practice he had opened in the summer of 1910. With family assistance, he had been commissioned to design a few rural buildings in Pomerania, but these contracts were insufficient to cover his running expenses. Gropius wrote hundreds of bids and proposals, receiving rejections to them all. In a letter to his lover and future wife, Alma Mahler, he complained that he was unable to "get excited about all this desk work, writing letters and negotiating. . . . This stupefying work is bad for me, mentally and physically."[25]

The factory in Alfeld—another commission facilitated by family connections—represented a breakthrough for Walter Gropius (1883–1969) and his partner Adolf Meyer (1881–1929), whom he had met in Behrens's studio. The Fagus project turned into a long-term contract that lasted until the end of their partnership in 1925; it also gives us abundant material with which we can reconstruct their artistic and creative development. Although Meyer's contribution to the design is difficult to trace with any specificity, his collaboration on the Fagus project is beyond doubt. This is borne out not only by the countless signatures on drawings for permit applications but also by Benscheidt himself.[26] Because Gropius conducted the negotiations as studio proprietor, enjoyed a presence in the media through the professional association and his lectures, and was furthermore very skilled at taking advantage of every opportunity for publishing his theoretical writings, his name tends to be mentioned more frequently—as is also the case here. The impression is that he was the sole creator of the building. However, at least with regard to architectural conceptualization, Meyer must be seen as having contributed in equal measure.[27] Meyer himself always considered the Fagus factory a collaborative effort between himself and Gropius, keeping a personal archive of nearly one hundred sheets of drawings.[28]

The Preliminary Project

At the beginning of February 1911, Benscheidt Sr. and Gropius met for the first time. Gropius suggested that he would create a design on the basis of a nonbinding offer. Should Benscheidt decide not to take the design, he would be under no obligation to pay and could forget the whole thing. Conversely, should he decide to use the design, an official commission would have to be issued and a fee commensurate with professional standards

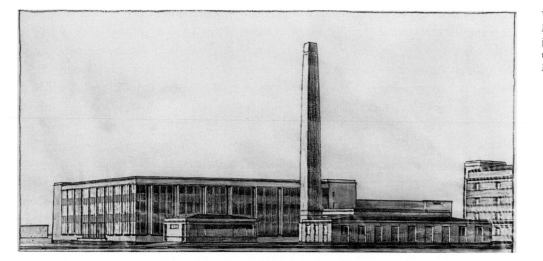

be agreed upon. Benscheidt accepted this proposal but insisted that the time spent on creating the design be paid regardless and asked Gropius to draft a preliminary project accordingly.[29]

A few days later, Gropius presented fundamental suggestions for change. He maintained that a satisfying architectural solution was only possible by "positioning the buildings at right angles" and thus "creating courtyard-like interstitial spaces."[30] By May 1911, Gropius was still presenting various proposals for relocating the clicking-knife department and he appears to have come close to persuading his client. In the end, however, Benscheidt rejected these proposals and also the idea of reversing the production line: "In the interest of the general impression one gains from a passing train, the following should also be considered: [as it stands,] the main elevation faces Behrens's factory. I would prefer the whole factory to be created as the mirror image of the current design. Then the attractive main elevation would be fully exposed toward Hanover. From a technical point of view, I can see no disadvantage."[31]

In fact, this proposal would have resulted in a much better visual impression of the building from a passing train because it was based on a long-distance effect of the main building oriented toward the open landscape. The argument—so unlike Benscheidt Sr. in that it was much too general and vague—that he "would have to put aside some practical considerations"[32] fails to convince. Rather, he seemed to be in favor of placing the main building directly opposite Behrens's factory—the constellation criticized by Gropius—because it was visually evocative of the competitive situation between the two companies.

To begin with, Benscheidt Sr. sent a full set of Werner's drawings to Gropius with the somewhat abrupt comment, "I ask you to check these plans to see what you can do about the facade."[33] Based on this material, Gropius and Meyer created two rough clay models in Berlin. The first one showed Werner's design; the other presented their own proposal for the Fagus factory. Neither the models nor photographs of the models have survived. However, Gropius later said that very few changes were made to the preliminary project and that "at least the main building was executed pretty much as it was originally conceived."[34]

This planning stage is revealed in a hitherto unknown perspective of the elevation facing the railroad.[35] It is most likely the "perspective sketch of the entire complex"[36] mentioned in a letter from the beginning of April, which had been completed in conjunction with the two clay models. At first glance, it does indeed seem to contain the main characteristics of the final design. The main building, for example, was already sketched in with the characteristic glazing rising continuously through three stories, the receding piers, and the unsupported glass corners. On the other hand, Gropius and Meyer combined the smaller buildings in the foreground on the railroad side (boiler house, wood-shaving bunker, and coal storage) into one uniform volume and chose a squared chimney, reminiscent of late classicist models, over the rounded chimney stack. On the whole, this plan exuded a latent classicism felt not only in the symmetry of the facade design but also in individual forms.

Upon closer inspection we can see, however, that the plan deviated considerably from the final, executed version with regard to the facade of the main building. In front of the parapets, two wide vertical buttresses per bay were closely related to Werner's lesene division. A watercolor blueprint from May 1911 labeled "sheet 1" and illustrating a window detail provides better insight into this planning stage. Incidentally, this is the earliest extant drawing from Gropius's architecture practice, not only for the Fagus project.[37] The vertical section shows that the piers were initially not intended to be battered back—as was later realized in the execution—but instead continued upward on the vertical. The recessed effect produced in the perspective drawing results from the projection of the coping, to which the windows are flat-joined, seeming to hang from it like curtain bands. Furthermore, the ground plan and elevation illustrate that the windows were to be connected to the pylons with skewed sheet-metal flashings—in other words, they should be read as independent casings or, in a manner of speaking, as oriels. In this approach, Gropius and Meyer were in tune with a design characteristic typical of pre–World War I office buildings; windows that project polygonally between multistory piers provide a vertical articulation that is interrupted only by breast walls in the form of sheet-plate aprons. One should remember, however, that this was a modern solution derived not from industrial architecture but from office buildings—as Gropius always referred to the main building in his correspondence with Benscheidt.

Windows of the main building, preliminary project, "sheet 1," May 1911.

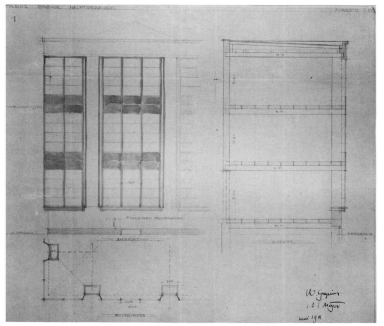

Before traveling to Berlin to take a look at the models created by Gropius and Meyer, Benscheidt Sr. requested a cost calculation based on Werner's plans; it showed an additional 100,000 marks over and above the building expenses. The Fagus GmbH shareholders refused to approve such an increase and Benscheidt Sr. felt compelled to drastically reduce the scale of the project. To lower expenses, he asked that the coal storage and the wood-shaving bunker be housed in one building. A smaller power house with a locomobile would be used instead of a stationary installation. This eliminated the need for a boiler house. The solid chimney gave way to an unfinished sheet-metal tube. One positive side effect of these modifications was that the lesser buildings on the railroad track side were now scaled down, offering not only a better view of the main building but also opening up an access lane between the factory and the tracks.

However, Benscheidt's decision to reduce the size of the production rooms had an even greater impact on the external image. The drying kilns as well as the production hall were reduced by one axis. This resulted in a shortening of the main building on the southeast side. Benscheidt even considered eliminating the third floor altogether, which would, however, have saved only 15,000 marks. Only Gropius's insistence persuaded the client to change his view on this point and to realize that "leaving out the third floor would make the building much less imposing. . . . I also believe that it will be a good advertisement and that alone will compensate for the additional cost."[38]

A compromise solution was found: to shorten the southeast wing to the point where the staircase begins and to house the packaging department in a single-story attached building. This decision—like the integration of the elevator tower into the compact building mass of the warehouse—was not only cost efficient but also served as a means of preparing for future expansions.

At the end of April 1911, when Benscheidt returned from his visit with Gropius and Meyer in Berlin, where he had inspected the models and perspective drawing, his first step was to consult Werner because he was concerned that the glazing in the main building would translate into a very considerable cost increase. In mid-May, Gropius delivered construction drawings, which were the basis for requesting quotes from various steel construction firms. Based on these estimates, Werner calculated that the cost difference between his own and the modified design would not exceed 15,000 to 20,000 marks. At this point, the option of a steel and glass facade was given serious consideration. In the end, Benscheidt accepted the preliminary project by Gropius and Meyer—with Werner's support, incidentally; he expressed his "unconditional approval"[39] of the drawings showing the elevation of

Elevation seen from railway. Photo by Edmund Lill, 1912.

the main building. The written agreement dated May 13, 1911, stipulated that Gropius must "make constructional decisions that will not make the building more expensive. At any rate, the additional costs . . . must not exceed those based on Mr. Werner's by more than 10,000."[40] With a total building cost of 400,000 marks, Benscheidt thought of this amount for the external design—which represented 2.5 percent of the total—as a good long-term investment because a modern building "will be a good advertisement for me."[41]

The Construction

Throughout the construction phase, Gropius and Meyer were under great pressure. This was largely due to the fact that Benscheidt Sr. had applied for building permission with Werner's plans at the end of April 1911. These still showed the old exterior design and the originally envisioned size of the complex. When a temporary building permit was granted on May 8, 1911, excavation and foundation work began on the basis of these plans. The cornerstone was laid on May 29, 1911. Far into July, the architects in Berlin worked feverishly at drawings, trying to keep up with each construction phase. Finally, toward the end of August, Gropius's plans were submitted to the building authorities as subsequent amendments.

The pace was driven by Benscheidt's desire to complete the construction before the onset of winter 1911–1912 and to begin production in the fall, if at all possible. The construction of a separate building for the forge and tool shop, in particular, was undertaken at great speed. Benscheidt installed several lathes and immediately began to produce both lasts and clicking knives in this temporary setup. When the scaffolding was removed from the building at the beginning of August, the client exclaimed enthusiastically how "extraordinarily simple and yet striking"[42] the architecture appeared.

The other buildings were completed on a priority basis. Benscheidt insisted, for example, that the sawmill be next in line so that he could install more workbenches for last production. Boiler house, warehouse, and drying kiln, on the other hand, were given lower

View from Hannoversche Strasse during construction, 1912.

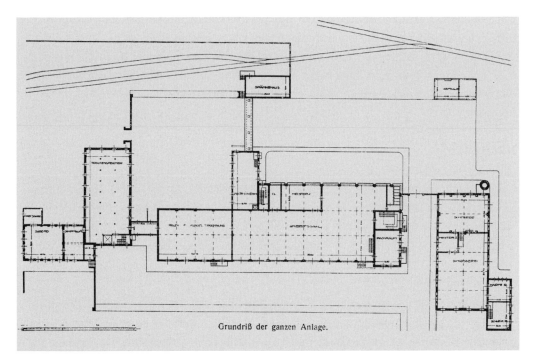

Grundriß der ganzen Anlage.

priority because these steps in the production process could be handled in the temporary sawmill set up in 1910 outside the Fagus factory site. Top priority was attached to the production hall, whose outfitting with machines and technical installations took longest. Benscheidt managed to handle the simultaneity of ongoing construction and production through rigorous organization. Soon, he was able to deliver to his curious customers and to close sales, although some difficulties were unavoidable.

The problems come through in the correspondence between Alfeld and Berlin. Gropius had not appointed a building manager and difficulties arising from this were soon apparent. Occasionally Werner and Benscheidt would make decisions on the spot, leaving Gropius and Meyer to play catch-up with their drawings. A constant stream of suggestions and demands for changes from Berlin added to the confusion. As some plans were incomplete, the bricklayers failed to execute the important 4–centimeter projection at the base; consequently, these sections were demolished and rebuilt.[43]

Things progressed at a slower pace, however, with regard to the glass facade of the main building, which posed a challenge to all participants. Benscheidt commissioned Hirsch, a company in Berlin, to deliver the steel construction for the glazed sections; during this period (spring–summer 1911), Hirsch was also delivering the windows for the small-motor factory of AEG. Structurally, the Alfeld building utilized standard steel profiles. Each bay featured three sections of floor-height glazing attached to the building's strucure on all four sides. The main building of the Fagus factory turned out to be a wonderful advertising vehicle not only for Benscheidt but also for Hirsch; in one advertising flyer, it is distinctively showcased.

The corner construction without piers—or, as Benscheidt called it, the "difficult corner"—required more detailed consultation.[44] The client requested a drawing with details of the roof and beam construction because the builders did not know how to attach the girders. Gropius sent a plan from the building engineering firm Heinrich Schütt in Hamburg, which he had "vetted and authorized."[45] The unattractive solution, still nicknamed the "Gropius knot" in the Fagus factory, demonstrates how unsure all those involved were in trying to solve the problem. When the main building was expanded in 1914, the knot was used again in the staircase, whose south and west corners do not have piers, although in this more finished area the knot is hidden behind a suspended ceiling.[46]

The Building

Gropius and Meyer were able to enforce only minor changes in the overall layout of the factory complex. Among these were slight adjustments in the disposition of individual building sections to create a more compact effect of mass. Overall, Werner's intended layout for the individual buildings within the complex was carried out; greater uniformity and coherence were achieved, however, through Gropius and Meyer's reductionism in form, material, and color.

The characteristic common to all Fagus buildings is a 40–centimter high, dark brick base that projects from the facade by 4 centimeters. The bricks are scorched, purplish-black, partially sintered fourth-grade remnants that Benscheidt purchased at a discount from his son-in-law's brickworks. Together with the black pointed masonry bond they create a continuous dark zone above which the light-colored buildings seem to float. The rising walls are faced in leather-yellow bricks—apparently third-grade bricks—whose irregular coloring animates the stone face.

Another stylistic characteristic of the Fagus factory is the sharp contouring of the cubical structures, in which the windows appear almost as cutouts. Orthogonal lines divide the external walls into planes and layers; the result is precision in form and visual commonality among the buildings. Thus an eaves seems to be continued in an adjacent building in a joint or translated into a brick course laid on edge that projects ever so slightly, with downspouts creating vertical boundaries. These "graphic" elements are meant to modulate the effect of light and shade, defining both the contour and the internal line of the building.

As did Eduard Werner's design, Gropius and Meyer's focused on the multifunctional main building. For consistency in the external image, they applied the 5–meter intervals used on the northeast side to the shorter southeast facade—that is, they deviated from the grid established with the production hall. Each wing was treated identically and the differentiated valuation of facades—still noticeable in Werner's design—fell away. Instead, the new aesthetic concept

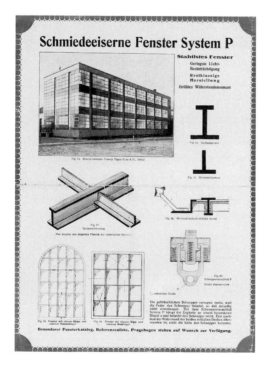

Advertising flyer for D. Hirsch, Berlin.

allowed for equal weight independent of function.

The vertical glazing rising through all three floors is still a striking feature of the main building. Subtle details make it appear like a suspended curtain wall. This impression is due mostly to the battered piers, a modification of the preliminary design, which result in a cuneiform shape that acts as a transition to the vertical bands of windows. This approach made the original plan of beveling the panes superfluous; now the panes could be connected to the piers at right angles. The windows no longer resembled oriels, instead, the emphasis of a surface plane made them appear like a three-story-high curtain wall. To increase this effect, the window frames were recessed by a mere 2 centimeters along the lintel and came to rest, as if on a beam, in front of the parapet on the ground floor. The cantilever effect was caused by a slight protrusion of the coping. Despite Gropius's comment to the contrary, which is too readily repeated in the critical literature, the main building of the Fagus factory does not have a curtain wall.[47] This is rather a glass membrane consisting of extremely large windows that reach from floor to ceiling.

The "Gropius knot." Ceiling construction in east corner.

The corner without piers, on the other hand, was a much more daring execution than the glazing. At the corners, the facade seems to bend in the middle of a bay at a right angle—literally wrapping itself around the building. Gropius and Meyer broke with the tradition, still present in Werner's design, holding that the design should consider the structurally weakest point of a building, securing it physically and reinforcing it visually. Instead, they reversed the principle: stability was replaced by a floating weightlessness, an effect enhanced by the dark base and the glazing above. Once again, the assumption has been that the construction was innovative—a steel frame or reinforced concrete. In fact, the building was constructed in a completely traditional manner whose technology was based on Werner's plans. This structure is a simple brickwork building, with an iron ceiling beam stretching between the plain battered piers and the rear wall of the building.[48]

While the clear-span corner of the main building has no visible support, a stair tower on the boundary of the glass facade obviously provides such support. The compact fabric of the tower, structured only with small, narrow windows, stands in clear contrast to the rest of the building. Rising above the coping and marked by a slight escarpment, it seems to lean like a stabilizing pillar against the glass-fronted main structure. Gropius and Meyer's preliminary design reveals that the main building was to be framed between this and a second, identical stair tower at the opposite end. The original idea can therefore be visualized as a long, low fabric surrounding the single-story sawtooth-roofed production hall, bent near the center of its extension and right in the middle of a bay, but stabilized at the ends—that is, at the actual corner points of the building.

In the final, scaled-down version of the Fagus factory, the main building is abruptly truncated, like a torso to which the single-story packaging building is attached without

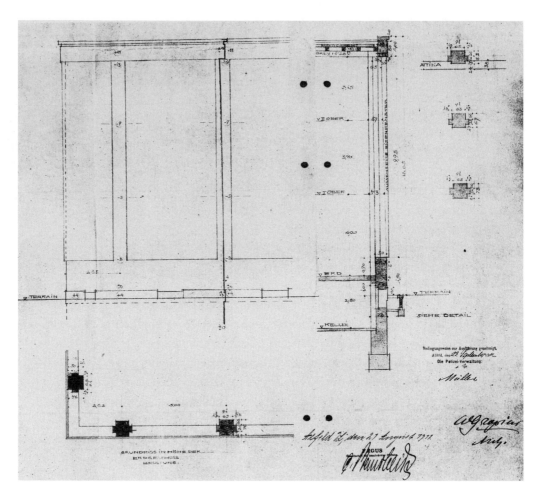

transition. The street elevation of this section has an unfinished look. What we see is a
temporary solution that needs to be expanded to achieve a final shape. This elevation cannot be called a facade in the sense of having a face. The few drawings of elevations, all
showing the view from the railroad, indicate that this side of the building was, perhaps,
never intended to have a specific face in the first place. Benscheidt, too, seems to have
interpreted the railroad side as his factory's main elevation; even Werner's sketches clearly
marked a front (railroad) elevation and a rear (street) elevation.

The verticality of the glass-clad main building contrasts with the horizontality of the
massive warehouse on the opposite side. Gropius and Meyer remained fairly true to
Werner's design; they did, however, specify that light-colored roughcast plastering be
used for the half-timbered building. The coarse texture created by the pebbles in the
plaster stands in deliberate contrast to the precision and polish of the brickwork in the
other buildings. The architects adeptly contained the volume of the massive building in a
precise and tranquil shape. The dark gray mansard roof with oblong, horizontally placed
roof shingles eases the visual height of the building, making it appear to have only four
stories.

The architecture of the Fagus factory operates with consistently uniform design elements that clearly mark the individual buildings as belonging together and yet create a
differentiation, even a hierarchy. This is expressed, for example, in the use of different win-

dow shapes. The large horizontal panes are reserved for the main structure, while the production hall, the sawmill, and the clicking-knife department are fitted with windows using a smaller and square pane.[49] On the other hand, the color scale of the materials acts as a unifying element throughout: yellow (brick), gray (slate roof, windows), black (base), and terra cotta (roof tiles).

View from Hannoversche Strasse, circa 1912.

Gropius and Meyer were also bound by contract to design the interior of the main building—that is, the offices on the second floor, which were open to the public. As in the architecture, here, too, few means were employed to maximum effect. The use of color, furniture, and fittings invested each room with a specific character and the sequential disposition set the stage in a psychologically perceptive manner.

To begin with, the customer or visitor was ushered into the waiting room, whose bright colors and informal wicker furniture created a friendly, relaxed impression. Met by one of the two directors or a director's assistant, they stepped into a long corridor. Glass partitions corresponding to the external windows of the main building offered views into the main office. In keeping with Benscheidt's philosophy, the office featured the latest in equipment and, like the production rooms, exuded an air of order, luminosity, and organization—a modern operation characterized by efficiency. Finally, the visitor entered into the collection or sample room, where products were displayed. The walls, painted in broad sweeps of strong colors, and the dark display cases created an almost solemn atmosphere.

Once visitors were convinced of the quality of the product, detailed talks were conducted in the executive offices. Both father and son Benscheidt always looked on factory tours as an important advertising tool and often undertook to guide the guests personally. In so doing, they were following an American example quite different in attitude from that of most German entrepreneurs, who tended to avoid allowing public access to their factories for fear of industrial espionage.[50]

The production hall was also carefully planned down to the smallest detail, although it was not singled out for special design treatment by the architects. The transmission belts and dust-extraction ducts were installed below the production hall (as they had been in Behrens's factory), creating clean, dust-free work conditions. Photographs of the interior show a layout virtually identical to the Behrens factory, with one difference: newer machines, set up in sequence with the production process. Daylight was also utilized more effectively in the Fagus hall.

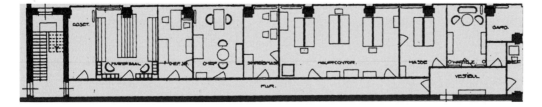

Main building, office floor with furniture, 1912.

Top: Main building,
office floor. Photo by
Edmund Lill, 1912.

Bottom: Production
hall. Photo by
Edmund Lill, 1912.

Benscheidt provided his workers with facilities that had become familiar: in the basement of the main building's short wing and underneath the shipping department he set up a cafeteria, a changing room with lockers, and washrooms. Because of his involvement in the Alfeld Building Cooperative, the manufacturer saw no reason to build separate estate housing for his workers, although Gropius may have made a suggestion to this effect. In a lecture and slide presentation at the beginning of April 1911 in Hagen, the architect showed a slide with the comment that it showed the "design for an American shoe-last factory near Hanover"—most likely the perspective view of the preliminary project he had just completed. The next slide showed the housing he had designed for the Janikow estate in Pomerania in 1909: "[How to create] corresponding workers' homes with inexpensive means."[51] The audience probably never realized that this was merely an idea. It is possible that Gropius wanted to present himself as an architect who was commissioned by an American and, hence, modern company to build not only the factory but also the factory workers' housing—surely an ideal but by no means innovative concept, as Werner's work alone had demonstrated.

During 1912, Gropius and Meyer also designed garages, a woodshed, a bicycle shed, the paving in the courtyard, the entrance gate, and the fence. Shortly after these tasks were completed, a long article on the Fagus factory appeared in the magazine *Der Industriebau*. Benscheidt thought that the article, richly illustrated with photographs, was "good advertisement"[52] and ordered 1,500 copies, which he distributed personally, and also asked his sales representatives to hand out to potential clients.

By December 1911, Benscheidt was able to send a full report to his American business partners. "As you know, it has been my goal to build as simply but also as clearly and accurately as possible, so that the exterior of the complex alone would proclaim that in this operation everything is geared toward precision. It is generally acknowledged that I have reached this goal, and the complex is very noticeable due to the excellent site."[53]

The Expansion

Precision distinguished the Fagus products from all others. In launching his new factory, Benscheidt focused on a single product—namely, shoe lasts for machine-made shoes and the corresponding clicking knives

Housing development for workers on the Janikow estate in Pomerania, 1909.

and cutting blocks. At the time, production methods in the shoe industry were constantly evolving and improving, and these products gradually turned into precision goods. In contrast to Behrens, who manufactured a wide range of products for the shoe-manufacturing trade, such as trade lasts, boot blocks, fullers, clamps, and shoe trees, Benscheidt concentrated on innovation and superior quality that would set industry standards and thus make him the leader in his field. To his American business partner, he wrote, "I hope to deliver for each part something different and something better."[54]

Benscheidt's calculations proved correct. Although he had to take some losses during his first year of operation, orders came in more quickly than he could meet in production. The factory shipped 1,500 lasts every day. But it was the Fagus clicking knives that were in greatest demand, and soon it was evident that the forge and the tool-and-die shop were too small. By the fall of 1912, only a year after production had begun under makeshift conditions, Benscheidt was discussing with his American business partners how to expand the clicking-knife department. His partners soon realized that the downsizing of the Fagus project, a decision made in the spring of 1911, had been a mistake and, in response, suggested that the entire complex should be expanded to twice its size. Once again they were willing to invest 800,000 marks.

The contract went directly to Gropius and Meyer, who would henceforth permanently replace Eduard Werner as architects for Fagus. From this point, all architectural tasks for the Fagus factory were handled directly by Gropius and Meyer. The first phase of the expansion began in October 1913. Parallel to the manufacturing process, the last-production buildings were to be renovated first. The additions were linked to the existing buildings—just as Werner had envisioned—as simple outbuildings with a southwest orientation—that is to say, facing the street. Benscheidt left the sawmill untouched for the time being and began with the warehouse. In February 1914, the production hall was expanded by three full axis-lengths. Finally, the main building was enlarged as well. The outbreak of the First World War on August 1, 1914, however, brought construction to a standstill virtually overnight. Benscheidt barely managed to get enough construction workers to finish the main building, which had been completed only up to the second floor; the interior finishing work had to be left until later. The building materials had been delivered for the clicking-knife department, but world events had overtaken everything else and there was no thought now to begin another expansion.

From an architectural point of view, the expansion of the complex was hardly challenging; all that needed to be done was to add length to existing buildings. Gropius and Meyer nevertheless seized the opportunity to improve the facade of the street elevation. A drawing, created no later than January 1914, illustrates the main motif in the design: the large glazed surface, previously unique to the main building, was now also applied to the clicking-knife

Expansion of warehouse and drying kilns. Factory photo, 1913

department and to the production hall. Although the low rectangles formed a more homogeneous and visually unified image, each building was treated differently. The tall main building, for example, was characterized by larger windowpanes, battered piers, and the corner without piers; the bays (consisting of 6 x 6 units) of the single-story production hall stretched across the piers like a continuous glass curtain; and the clicking-knife department seemed to be a combination of both treatments: these were variations of the theme established in the main building.

Gropius and Meyer created a true masterpiece in the street-side facade of the main building. The original concept, captured in the preliminary project and in an elevation published in 1913, was still based on the pylon solution with the two stairwell towers at either end. In the revised version, the architects arrived at a convincing new form: the glass facade was wrapped around the south corner as well and on the third floor it was bent again without visible support at the west corner. All that remained of the pylon was a two-story-high brick wall positioned into the face off center that drew attention to the main entrance. The brick wall was articulated with horizontal shadow joints, finely attuned to the gridwork, which in turn bent sharply at the west corner and continued along part of the rear facade of the main building. This wall created an important visual division between production and administration; it separated the workers' entrance to the basement from the stairs that led to the main entrance and, hence, to the office floor.

Perspective drawing of extension, planning status January 1914.

The most inspired gesture, however, was the placement of the staircase in the trussless south corner. The building seemed to defy the laws of gravity and the landings, too, seemed to be suspended in thin air. Here Gropius and Meyer achieved an "aesthetic and architectural coup *par excellence*."[55] They had already experimented in a design, realized only a few months previously, for the so-called Model Factory for the Werkbund Exhibition in Cologne in 1914. Gropius and Meyer still adhered to a design featuring a long building framed by staircases at either end, although these were already entirely conceived in glass—in a partial reversal of the original concept for Alfeld—thus giving the facade, articulated with the piers, the impression of a solid wall. The round staircases, with steps projecting freely from the newel, were transformed into a square variation in the Alfeld construction and the full glazing of the semicircle in the model factory corresponded to the three-sided glazing (at least on the third floor) of the corners without supports.

Left: South corner of main building with staircase. Photo by Albert Renger-Patzsch, April 1928. Fagus series no. 7.

Right: Staircase of Model Factory for Werkbund Exhibition, Cologne. Photo by Hugo Schmölz, 1914.

Gropius and Meyer insisted that the model factory be built from "real" materials and not, as was the case for nearly all other buildings in the Werkbund Exhibition in Cologne, as ephemeral architectural models. Several companies from the Rhineland donated the building materials in return for a mention in the official catalog. One of these was the Düsseldorf company Fenestra, a steel-frame construction firm, which provided the window construction. It is reasonable to assume that this generous donation was linked to Benscheidt's placement of an order with the company for the windows of the main building expansion of the Fagus factory. The Fenestra system was fundamentally different than the standard profiles used during the first building phase in 1911.[56] The most important innovation lay in the different width measurements, with the vertical bars much thinner than the horizontal muntins. As Gropius continued to maintain decades later, his goal had been to achieve an even greater "etherealization."[57]

The War Years

Benscheidt was able to expand the Fagus factory only marginally during the years of the First World War. While Gropius immediately joined the reserve unit of his regiment when war broke out, Meyer found an interesting occupation in the design department of the renowned steel manufacturer Breest & Co., work that was considered essential to the war effort and that released him from military service. From Berlin, Meyer oversaw the completion of the main building in Alfeld and updated the expansion plans readied in 1914 for those buildings that had not yet been begun.

Once the production rooms were expanded and the lathes installed, the locomobile could no longer deliver sufficient power and had to be replaced with a more powerful

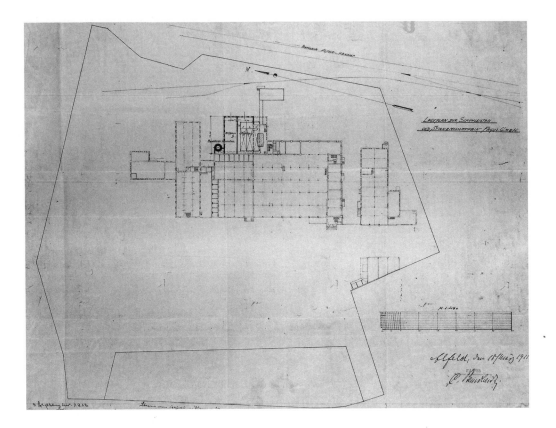

machine. This led to the expansion of the boiler house and the construction of a separate power house. At the outbreak of war, the excavation was still underway and construction had to be postponed. This caused great difficulties for Benscheidt because frequent locomobile breakdowns often paralyzed production and led to considerable loss in revenue.

Acquiring a new machine during the war was extremely difficult. Therefore, in the summer of 1915, Benscheidt decided to first construct the chimney stack, which would become a distinctive feature of the complex as a whole. Dark horizontal stripes "in chocolate-colored iron clinker bricks"[58] accentuated the over 30–meter-high round stack built of leather-yellow brick up to the roofline of the main building. As the instruction to "replicate the grooves from the warehouse"[59] in one drawing indicates, these stripes served to integrate the stack into the overall graphic image of the architecture. Above the height of the main building, the solid encasement dissolves into brown piers that support a cylindrical water tank faced in the same iron clinker bricks. Beyond, one can see the actual chimney, which passes through the water tank in a steep ascent. This highly effective design, which differentiates between encasure and stack, invested the chimney with a distinctive corporeality. Different design variations from July 1914 are witness to the effort put into designing the stack. In one drawing, a sketch beneath the main image presents a solution with louver-like concrete supports whose delicate form is reminiscent of the furniture Gropius and Meyer were creating during the same period.

At the end of 1915, construction finally began on the power house. For this section, too, several drawings exist for different phases dated June 1914 and modified in March 1915 by Meyer. The drawings all have one main feature in common: floor-height glazing that was wrapped around at least one, if not several, corners of the building. These design elements

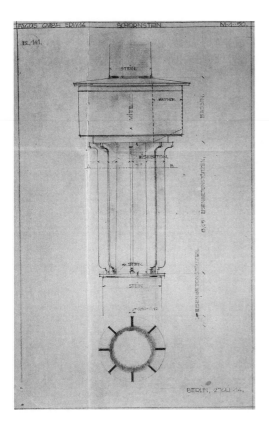

Design variation for chimney, 1914.

would become the dominant characteristics of all Fagus buildings. While they were initially reserved for the main building, we can see that in the expansion after 1914 these elements were applied to the production hall, the tool-and-die shop, and, finally, the power house. They were used subsequently in the buildings that followed during the 1920s.

Benscheidt chose the design from 1914—in a slightly enlarged form—where the power house is glazed on two sides. An argument against using the fully glazed facades for the boiler house may have been the high room temperature and, hence, the increased thermal pressure on the iron-framed windows, which would have led to rapid deterioration. To avoid disrupting day-to-day production, the new boiler house was built around the old one, which still housed the locomobile. Once the power house was completed and the new power machine hooked up, the old boiler house could be demolished.[60]

In contrast to the other buildings constructed on the site up to this point, the power house was a steel frame structure with a support in the glazed corner section. As in the main building, the glass surfaces consisted of window elements with 4 x 4 panes in a flush rectangle, whereby each two elements were arranged one above the other. In the upper row, they continued as a band of windows that aligned with the skylight of the adjoining boiler house. Photographs shot in the winter of 1918–1919 show this area still covered with wood paneling and temporary windows. The temporary arrangement was the result of Benscheidt's decision to wait until after the end of the war before purchasing a second boiler. The building was fully completed only in 1921–1922, after the large machine had finally been incorporated.

Photographs taken in the 1930s show how well this building fit into the overall composition. The glazed corner section of the power house was positioned to be seen from passing trains coming from Hanover. At the same time, it created cohesion: from the horizontal block of the warehouse, the onlooker's glance was automatically drawn to the tall chimney, then past the single-

Side facing the railroad track with temporary boiler house. Factory photo, winter 1918–1919.

story glazed power house and through the transparent skylight of the boiler house and back to the main building; the low clickinging knife department, ending in the vertical of the second chimney, provided the final accent. In analogy to the power house, passengers traveling from Göttingen saw the glazed east corner of the main building framed by the distinctive markers of the chimneys.

The animated fluctuation in height, the change between horizontal structure and vertical rhythms, heavy closed volumes and light dissolved fabrics, are indicators of an approach that deliberately utilized contrasts while arriving at a harmony of opposites in a manner best expressed as a pictorial or visual structure created from the perspective of the railroad tracks. This effect was achieved mostly through harmonious proportions and subtle interactions among details. In contrast to Eduard Werner, Gropius and Meyer did not simply string one building after another based on function; instead, they integrated each component into a visual unity.

The street elevation of the complex created a similar, although much less animated, impression. It, too, was developed parallel to passing traffic, but followed a continuous straight line in contrast to the railroad elevation. The volumes of the warehouse, production hall, and main building clearly distinguished from one another by their difference in height, were artfully linked so that even from this perspective one can speak of a pictorial composition. In contrast to its condition after the first building phase, this elevation was much improved by the expansion in 1913–1914, which gave its facade an aesthetic value equal to that on the railroad side.

From the selection of photographs for promotional publications, it is clear that Benscheidt Sr. always thought of the view from the railroad tracks as the main facade—undoubtedly driven by his rivalry with Behrens, but also influenced by the general tendency at the time to regard rail transport as the primary means of transportation, and not only in industry. Gropius and Meyer, on the other hand, showed great foresight in allow-

Finished power house and boiler house. Photo by Edmund Lill, November 1922.

ing for future developments in automobile trends and designed the facade overlooking the street accordingly. At the same time, they gave something to the complex that it had lacked until then: a clear link to the main entrance, visually and physically directing visitors to the administration building and, thus, to management.

After Meyer was conscripted in the spring of 1915, the architects were no longer able to supervise construction. In the building permit application for the new power house, Benscheidt explained that Gropius had been unable to sign the plans because he was serving in the army; at the same time, the manufacturer assured the authorities that Gropius had "dictated the ideas for the layout of the complex and checked the drawings."[61] Gropius confirmed this statement indirectly in a letter he wrote in the summer of 1916 from the battlefield to his mother, who was staying with her daughter's family in Alfeld. "When you have a moment, take the children to see Fagus; a lot has been done there during the war. I am in constant contact by correspondence and am directing the project to the best of my abilities from here."[62] Wherever possible, work was postponed until after the war.

The Fagus factory as seen from a passing train. Factory photos, 1930s.

The Fagus factory was perpetually a construction site from 1911 to 1918. Some of the temporary solutions instituted then were still in place well into the 1980s because the building expansion, begun during World War I, was never completed during the 1920s. The war also delayed publication of the photographs that showed the expanded complex. Hence, critics and historians "discovered" the Fagus factory only in the late 1920s, when Benscheidt's philosophy began to bear fruit; the building provided him not only with good advertisement, it also made his firm known worldwide.

Industrial Architecture as Art

Monumental Art and Industrial Building

At the beginning of 1914, architecture critic Adolf Behne noted: "One can say without exaggeration that today's new industrial buildings capture the interest of the public and of critics like nothing else. A factory that fails to meet artistic demands is judged mercilessly, more so than an unimaginative town hall or a poorly executed monument. Ten years ago, it was still possible to build any which way and no one took any note."[1]

But even prior to World War I, renowned architects were frequently asked to design utilitarian or industrial buildings. From the middle of the nineteenth century onward there was a strong movement in Germany to apply artistic design to production sites in large industrial complexes.[2] This trend was motivated, on the one hand, by the desire to integrate factory complexes into a landscape or specific environment and, on the other hand, by the economic importance and distinct self-image of the companies in question.

After the Gründerjahre (Foundation Period 1871–1873), architecture was used deliberately for commercial purposes; conspicuous factory buildings—such as breweries in the shape of castles—made a lasting impression on consumers. The Yenidze cigarette factory in Dresden is a well-known example of this type of architecture. Built in 1907, its mosquelike shape alluded to the exotic provenance of the tobacco that was processed in it. "Day and night, during profitable and unprofitable business hours, this building is an advertisement for the owner, at no cost to the publicity account."[3]

Left: Yenidze cigarette factory, Dresden. Architect: Martin Hammitzsch, 1907.

Opposite: South corner of main building. Photo by Albert Renger-Patzsch, April 1928. Fagus series no. 8a.

Peter Behrens's work and architecture for the giant electrical concern, AEG, on the other hand, went far beyond such superficial notions. With his appointment in 1907 as artistic consultant, Behrens became responsible for creating an all-around image for the international company; he designed the trademark, all printed matter, a full range of household appliances, the factory buildings, the exhibition architecture, all retail store installations, and staff clubhouses and their interior design as well as workers' housing. In short, a unifying artistic vision and coherence that built identity—a precursor to what we now call corporate identity.

The Werkbund, founded in Germany in 1907, took these already inclusive design requirements and transferred them into a national economic program. Leaders in politics, trade, publishing, and art—Peter Behrens was one of the founding members—joined at the highest level for mutual support and practical application. Their goal was to produce innovative, high-quality consumer commodities that would be compatible not only in the domestic market but also succeed as export products. The idea was to seize market shares from the two leading economies at the time, England and France, while fostering a new national pride in high-quality work.

The business community soon realized that architecture expressing innovation and quality could be an effective tool for advertising. In addition to conspicuous buildings, whose advertising character was all too blatant, tastefully designed buildings with an air of dignity and refinement began to appear. Artistic flair was seen as an outward expression of the internal status and superiority of the firm. This approach was especially welcome to companies dealing in capital goods that were unable to employ direct product promotion.

Peter Behrens's ambition to raise factory architecture to the status of "industrial neoclassicism," which he had promoted with the AEG buildings, was soon adopted by the Werkbund in Berlin. This *"neudeutsche"* (new German[4]) monumental architecture

AEG turbine factory, Berlin. Architect: Peter Behrens, 1908–1909.

expressed more than just the economic status of the company; it was an embodiment of industry's role as the primary force behind nationhood and social change. Behrens's "purified" neoclassicism was complemented by simplified forms. His buildings were characterized by precision and a clean stereotomy. A compact contour, exactness in details, and durable materials evoked magnitude, power, and austerity—all characteristics of a new monumental style founded on the conditions of industrial work. Economy in contour was also an expression of an economic exploitation of raw material; the placement of identical building components in a row echoed the principle of mass production.

Formulas of what is dignified, adopted from the history of architecture, were added to the architectural vocabulary based on the functional character of a factory. Thus Behrens designed the facade of the Turbine factory (1908–1909) in the manner of a temple front; in other words, he elevated the profane to a sacred status. This tendency to ennoble the profane was a recurring theme in Behrens's work, as in the AEG pavilion for the shipbuilding fair in Berlin in 1908, inspired by the octagonal ground plan of the Palatine Chapel in Aachen. What we see is, however, more than an eclectic transfer of style; this was a novel and contemporary interpretation of familiar patterns. A near-abstract reduction to essential elements, it created new symbols for a modern world driven by technology. History and industry were made visible in the merging of symbolic form and modern material. In the vertical plane of the window and in the polygonal tympanum of the Turbine factory, Behrens's contemporaries recognized both a hammer standing upright on its handle and an archaic Doric column.[5]

Working with Behrens, Walter Gropius (June 1908 to March 1910) and Adolf Meyer (November 1907 to September 1908) experienced firsthand how the design for the Turbine factory was developed (from fall 1908 to spring 1909). At first, the young architects identified with their master, but soon both entered into a phase of critical examination. The catalyst for their criticism, Gropius later said, was that "neither the front of the Turbine factory nor the facade on Volta Strasse, a small-motor factory, were structurally 'true' but seemed instead [to be] aesthetically manipulated."[6] In fact, the main building of the Fagus factory can be interpreted as an architectural revision of the Turbine factory, with Gropius and Meyer taking an "antithetically dependent" stand against Behrens.[7]

AEG pavilion for shipbuilding exhibition, Berlin. Architect: Peter Behrens, 1908.

They proceeded to correct their teacher's approach virtually by inversion. While Behrens had placed the supports vertically on the longitudinal side and slanted the windows between the supports, Gropius and Meyer slanted the piers and fastened the multistory glass skin perpendicularly to the lintel. This aspect of their design still echoed the main facade of the Turbine factory with its pylons and the glass apron, which seemed to be suspended from the gable. Behrens had created solid and accentuated corner sections. His students, however, took the opposite approach and designed fully glazed corners without visible supports or pylons.

In the Turbine factory design, Behrens treated structural issues by slanting the non-load-bearing facade components inward. This resulted in a convincing solution for the glazing on the longitudinal side but turned out to be less successful when applied to the concrete piers. These were simply placed in front of the three-hinged arch construction of the hall, while the gable was, in fact, supported by the glass-curtained facade. Here, convention and the architect's *"Kunstwollen"* (artistic urge) overrode construction. The reinforced corner delivered not only a sense of stability but, together with the tympanum, it also invested the building with a monumentality that was charged with pathos.

Despite their enthusiasm for Behrens, the pathos invoked criticism from the younger generation. In 1913, Adolf Behne stated that Behrens "puts a little too much emphasis on weight, mass, and monumentality. At times his simplifications are almost crude. He turns industry into a Cyclops, a giant incapable of subtlety."[8] The Fagus factory architecture distinguished itself even in this: it avoided megalomaniac gestures or exaggerated symbolism. The corners without piers enhanced the already striking visual lightness of the main building. But they, too, were no more structurally true than Behrens's solution and were realized, not without difficulty, within the constraints of the prescribed brickwork construction.

Gropius and Meyer's attitude toward monumentality was ambivalent. Behrens stated that, for Gropius, monumental art was connected to "a remote violence, in front of which we fall to our knees; it makes us shiver and its size overpowers our soul."[9] But the architecture of Gropius and Meyer did not exude this kind of power. Instead, their work had more in common with the definition that Gropius elaborated in his writings, which called for internal rather than external dimension manifest in a closed contour, in the physicality of the volume, and in harmonious proportions. In addition to lightness, it is precisely this type of corporality, far removed from ostentation and symbols of power, that made the main Fagus building at Alfeld one of the seminal buildings of the International Style.

With the Turbine factory in mind, we can look afresh at the street elevation of the main building in Alfeld. Once again, Gropius and Meyer repeated not only the corner without piers, they also applied the horizontal design of Behrens's pylons to the pylon remnant that was recessed into the thickness of the wall while reducing the height—so to speak, a twofold revision of Behrens's design. In 1911, Gropius confirmed Behrens's earlier observation that the mortise joints served to emphasize the non-load-bearing function of this building section—in Alfeld, this was amply evident.[10] At the same time, the mortise joints created a link between the two facades. As in the Turbine factory, the joints echoed the sightline of the crossbars in the adjacent window segments.

The Fagus commission inspired Gropius to study the topic of factory architecture more closely. The outcome was a lecture entitled "Monumental Art and Industrial Building," presented on April 10, 1911, at the Folkwang Museum in Hagen.[11] The institution had been founded by Karl Ernst Osthaus, a financier and patron of artists, especially of Henry van de Velde and Peter Behrens, and also one of the leading members of the Deutscher Werkbund. Gropius met Osthaus in the spring of 1908 and gained much from this new acquaintance: a personal referral to Behrens, admittance to the Deutscher Werkbund in

December 1910, and, in March of the following year, a commission to assemble a collection of photographs documenting excellence in industrial building for the Deutsches Museum für Kunst in Handel und Gewerbe (German Museum for Art in Trade and Production), founded by Osthaus and supported by the Werkbund.[12]

Gropius's slide lecture in Hagen was aimed at entrepreneurs. Benscheidt Sr., who soon afterward joined the Deutsches Museum für Kunst in Handel und Gewerbe, is said to have been in the audience that night.[13] In this lecture, Gropius laid the foundation for his publications on the topic of industrial architecture, which were to follow between 1911 and 1914. Gropius's texts are essentially identical to Behrens's; in some instances, he not only followed the original ideas very closely, he even reprised some passages verbatim.[14] What was different, however, was his thorough study of how modern factory architecture influenced working conditions. On this subject, Gropius was in favor of top-down reform, which he felt could help resolve social issues and prevent a revolution. With his patriarchal business philosophy, Benscheidt Sr. may well have been a source of inspiration to Gropius.

Gropius began to be acknowledged as an expert in industrial building. Publishing his theories in an international center, compiling the photograph collection on excellence in industrial building, and designing the 1914 model factory in Cologne all contributed to establishing his reputation. Within a few years, he had climbed to the top, joining the elite of the Werkbund, whose opinions helped shape not only his theories but also his self-image as an artist/architect.[15] The buildings by Gropius and Meyer, the latter having joined the Werkbund in 1912, grew out of this environment.

In 1913, critic Adolf Behne divided the new industrial architecture into three categories. Their common characteristic, he said, was "a sincere devotion to the importance and value of industrial needs"[16]—in other words, their expression must be founded in purpose and not cloaked in the disguise of a borrowed style. The differences between individual modern architects, Behne continued, were to be found in how they interpreted "nature, value, and the soul of industry." He categorized Peter Behrens as a representative of "pathos" (AEG Berlin buildings), Richard Riemerschmid as a "romantic" (Deutsche Werkstätten für Handwerkskunst, Hellerau), and Hans Poelzig as a "logician" (Chemische Fabrik, Luban), all the while making it clear that he found Poelzig's rational approach most appealing.

Gropius and Meyer were not mentioned. Behne subsequently included them among the representatives of "pathos. . . . Peter Behrens's influence on industrial architecture is great. Anyone will recognize an individual voice, for example, in the works of someone like Gropius (Fagus Shoe Last Factory in Alfeld) and yet one cannot ignore the relationship to Behrens's work."[17] Behne stressed the "industrial classicism" that was so pronounced in Behrens's work, but more subdued in Gropius's and Meyer's, where it should be understood more as stylistic conformity.

We have become accustomed to focus on the antithetical, or the contrast to Behrens, as the modern element of the Fagus factory. This has somewhat obliterated the fact that this architecture was nevertheless closely related to its predecessor and yet experienced as strongly avant-garde by Gropius's contemporaries (in spite of or perhaps because of this dependence). This perception was largely founded in the fact that, from the 1920s onward, any resemblance to historic styles was thought of as negative. For the same reason, it has been difficult to understand the more obvious references to neoclassicism in the Werkbund model factory. However, these are present in the Fagus factory, above all when we focus not only on the main building but also on the other structures in the complex. The 1914 sawmill expansion facing the railroad tracks, for example, is essentially a portico projected into the plane and reduced to pillar, architrave/frieze, and triangular gable. This design feature marked the building behind the warehouse as the production entrance through which the raw material was brought into the factory.

Sawmill, facade overlooking railroad tracks. Factory photo, 1930s.

One must remember that the Fagus factory wasn't "discovered" until the late 1920s,[18] made famous by the photographs taken of the expansion during the Weimar Republic. But the series featured the main building and the glass walls, giving little attention to the aspect of industrial neoclassicism.

Antiquity

The importance of antiquity—that is to say antiquity conveyed through neoclassicism—is evident in Gropius and Meyer's work prior to 1914, followed by a final flicker in 1921–1922, after a brief excursion into expressionism. For industrial architecture, the reference turned out to be more abstract, related to the general principle rather than to a concrete form. But even when they were faced with building tasks that called for traditional representational formulas, Gropius and Meyer refused to resurrect the past; pillared facades, triangular gables, Ionic capitals were so drastically reduced that they no longer echoed any identifiably classic model.

Although Gropius and Meyer entered into a critical dialog with the work of Behrens— a dialog that continued beyond the Turbine and the Fagus factories, respectively—their work was related to that of their teacher's in that they practiced the new monumental style whose creative source lay in a rapprochement between industry and antiquity. For Gropius, at least, the issue was far more tangible than an abstract artistic principle. Instead, it expressed his attitude to life, as we can see in his private letters to Alma Mahler (circa 1910), which touch on the themes of antiquity/neoclassicism and work/industry.

The breadth of these ideas is evident in a manuscript that Gropius composed in the early summer of 1910. It was entitled "On the Nature of Different Artistic Urge in the Orient and the Occident."[19] In this essay, Gropius examined Alois Riegl's definition of "artistic urge."[20] Riegl opposed Gottfried Semper's theory, which stipulated purpose, raw material, and technique as the driving forces in art. To Riegl, these forces were no more than "coefficients of friction," subsumed to the will of the artist as a spiritual principle arising from prevailing circumstances. Or, as Gropius put it, "Matter in and of its own is dead and without character. It draws life only from the form that the creative will of the artist breathes into it."[21]

Gropius further posited that human artistic urge would always oscillate between two extremes: antiquity/Orient and baroque/Indo-Germanic, indicating that these definitions should be interpreted not only from an art-historical perspective but in the broadest sense. "The first gives rise to a simple differentiated order, which follows chaos—the second, on the other hand, to an order that is too differentiated and is closer to chaos. The perfect balance, the most differentiated order (Greek antiquity), lies in the middle."[22]

The massive architecture of antiquity, Gropius continued, achieved its impact because "two sections are removed from the fabric, like sunken grooves and fluting, while maintaining the organic integrity of the whole. The architectural movements in the fabric occur in a tactile plane (for two-dimensional areas [ornament] on a tactile line). The secret to achieving a compact impression lies in this law of the envelope, as I like to call it."

To illustrate his theory, Gropius sketched a facade from a ground-plan perspective, with

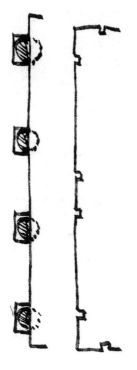

Facade models:
Renaissance and Antiquity.
Sketch by Walter Gropius,
1910.

half-columns placed along its front—the most popular means, during the Renaissance, of adding mass. Next to it, he sketched the model for a massive building in the classic style with some parts removed; in principle, this second model corresponds to the main building of the Fagus factory, where the supports are recessed into the building fabric.

In 1913, Fritz Hoeber pointed out how important Riegl's term, "tactile plane" was in Behrens's design of the Turbine factory.[23] He recognized it in the relief-like division of the surfaces, in how the projecting components related to the ground area, and in the grooves as connecting lines—that is to say, the graphic system, as we have called it in the context of Fagus. By uncovering layers and defining coherent planes, shadow effects were created that structured the building and gave it a certain amount of plasticity. They also allowed for a clear visual reading from a distance.

Gropius was convinced that "the silhouette will . . . become a modern concept in architecture, for the increasing speed in transportation and of life in general forces the eye to be satisfied with perception on a superficial level and hence, automatically, with a reduction to the simplest, sensual impressions (retardation of dimensions). We seem to be turning away from the baroque back toward antiquity."[24]

Based on Riegl's theory for classifying late antique art, Gropius came up with an interpretation of where art stood in 1910: chaotic eclecticism was giving way to a new direction in art. In a letter to Alma Mahler, he wrote, "Until now, romantic art has been a triumph of intellect over natural instinct or, rather, a degenerate intellect that put the emotional world into chains. What we have to strive for is a harmony between these two worlds, a new classicism, turning back from a superculture to a more animalistic, less meaningful existence."[25] In these early years, Gropius tended to think in pairs of opposites in his search for harmony between extremes, a harmony that was, in his mind, absolutely linked to antiquity. In his correspondence with Mahler, he mentioned how the ancient Greeks had equated "a beautiful spirit with a beautiful body, and I religiously adore this duality. You will understand how this applies figuratively to art."[26]

The secret power of proportion was understood as the essential tool for creating harmony. Gropius and Meyer worked with systematic design principles based on grid figurations that sometimes followed the Golden Section.[27] Beyond this, psychological factors of perception played an important role. These optical tricks were usually meant to enhance the intended effect. One such trick in the main Fagus building was the greater width of the horizontal transoms in relation to the vertical stanchions or, as Helmut Weber noted, the wider window panels in the trussless corners, which enhanced the impression of lightness.[28] The greater height of the window panels for the upper floors compensated for the deficiencies of the human eye.[29] It is therefore no surprise that, even in his old age, Gropius would still say of the Parthenon, "In it, intuition and intellect combine to triumph over the deficiencies of the human eye. This is true architecture."[30]

The architecture of the Fagus factory was an expression of this search for the rhythmic, antique conception of massive architecture, representing the most differentiated ideal, a search for harmony between art and industry. This does not mean, however, that the main building should be seen as a throwback to classical temples, even though, in his correspondence with Benscheidt in 1911 and later, in his old age, Gropius used classic terminology to describe the individual components of the building: pillar, column, architrave, frieze, and coping. If factory architecture is to be included in the genealogy of modernism, it would be better—in the case of Gropius and Meyer's Fagus factory—to speak of such architecture as a new monumental embodiment of the antique conception of massive architecture.

America

Ever since the turn of the previous century, "the land of limitless possibilities,"[31] years ahead of Europe in its development through progressive technology, efficiency, and limitless growth, had become synonymous with modernity. North America achieved this lead through abundant natural resources and fertile soil as well as a "pioneer spirit of objectivity." Everything exceeded ordinary dimensions: cities, houses, factories, traffic, and nature.

Many travel accounts published in Germany perpetuated this image of America and their popularity speaks of the public's keen interest. New York, the quintessential metropolis, was the point of arrival for travelers to the New World. Next, they would visit Niagara Falls to admire not only this spectacle of nature but also the power station where the awe-inspiring natural energy was harnessed. After 1912, the Ford car factory in Detroit (Highland Park) was included in the sightseeing program, as were, sometimes, the steelworks in Pittsburgh. Returning travelers reported on these sights with a mixture of awe and admiration. They also marveled at the fully automated mail-order house of Sears Roebuck in Chicago and at the latest inventions from Thomas A. Edison's "secret laboratories." At the time, Edison was described as the "most phenomenal human being today."[32] Returning to New York, travelers focused their attention on the big city and its skyscrapers. Neither art nor culture featured in their program, which centered instead on civilization and feats of engineering.

Among the attractions in the cities on the Great Lakes were the gigantic grain elevators and silos. While few stopped to actually tour a silo, all gazed upon them in astonishment from the passing train. "There they stand . . . these huge gray pipes, fourteen, fifteen of them, one next to the other like cartridges in the cartridge pouch of a god. . . . These grain elevators are like skyscrapers. They remind me of the generators at the power stations at Niagara Falls. The live force of the earth is gathered in them, the fulfilled hope of the millions who stream into the country."[33]

It was Walter Gropius who included the silos, previously presented mostly in travel books and engineering magazines, in the discussion on architecture. He may have begun to collect photographs not only of American but also of German grain elevators as early as 1910. Some of these images were shown for the first time during his lecture on monumental art and industrial building at Hagen in April 1911. They were also included in the collection for excellence in industrial building for the Deutsches Museum für Kunst in Handel und Gewerbe and published in the 1913 yearbook of the Deutscher Werkbund to illustrate Gropius's essay, "The Development of Modern Industrial Architecture."[34]

Until the outbreak of World War I, Gropius collected not only photographs of American silos but also of factories that he perceived as particularly modern. Karl Osthaus was a great help, as he had incorporated photographs of American industrial buildings into the collection "Modern Architecture" as early as 1910. Osthaus also took advantage of his good contacts with many leading personalities in the United States to acquire other photographs for Gropius—many taken from advertising brochures.[35]

Alma Mahler, who stayed in New York from October 1910 to March 1911, also sent Gropius "architectural things" and "arch. brochures [*sic*]."[36] This may be what he referred to in a letter to Osthaus on February 2, 1911: "I have recently received images of some new and very beautiful American concrete buildings, which you may not know; . . . naturally, I'll be glad to make them available for inclusion in the collection."[37] These reproductions may, however, not necessarily have been acquired in the United States, for some of the six photographs of American silos, shown during the Hagen lecture at the beginning of April 1911, were taken from German periodicals on structural engineering.[38]

Hardly a month went by in 1911 when Gropius did not report to Osthaus the receipt of new American examples. In some instances, he ran into the same problems he had previously encountered with German sources, for "from America, people are sending me photographs that completely miss the mark. They are abominable; people simply don't understand that plain, utilitarian buildings can be beautiful."[39]

Father and son Benscheidt also assisted Gropius in his search. At the time he was drafting the designs for Fagus, Gropius received several postcards of buildings from Benscheidt Sr., but these were unlikely to have been images of American silos or factories.[40] A year later, the situation changed. In August 1912, Benscheidt Jr. helped Gropius to find American photographs for the collection on excellence in industrial building, which was presented as a traveling exhibition in several German cities. To a friend working at the National Association of Manufacturers in New York, the younger Benscheidt wrote: "The architect who designed our factory building would like photographs of the following American factories: (1) the Brown Hoisting Machinery Company, New York, 50 Church St., [which] has executed several large buildings; (2) the complex of the St. Louis Portland Cement Works; (3) silos of the Washburn Crosby Society in Buffalo, Minneapolis, and in other cities; (4) Dakota Elevator in Buffalo (especially important). The architect wants to use these photographs for an exhibition and therefore they should be as large as possible and very focused, so that they could be enlarged to a size of 45 x 60 cm. Expense is not an issue."[41]

Gropius already had photographs of two of the buildings on this list. His goal was to track down better photographs for the purpose of publication and exhibition. Both Benscheidt Sr. and Jr. continued, well into the 1920s, to inform their architect of silos that were brought to their attention.

What fascinated Gropius about utilitarian architecture in North America was their simplicity directly derived from purpose. "Their architectural face has such import that a visitor immediately understands with convincing power what the purpose of the building is."[42] According to his classification system from 1910, they represented the "simple differentiating order" that he had labeled "antiquity/Orient," the first phase of a development characterized by the rough-hewn forms of a new trend. Riegl included Egyptian architecture in this category, where "windows . . . are omitted because they would have been distracting holes in the closed tactile form; doors, a necessary evil, are used as sparingly as possible. On the outside, the Egyptian temple with its undivided walls appears to the world like a tactile unit."[43]

Gropius's reaction resulted in an often quoted statement, "With their monumental expressive power, the grain elevators of Canada and South America, the coal silos of the great railway companies, and the modern factory halls of the North American industrial trust can be compared to the buildings of ancient Egypt."[44] The pylons that Gropius and Meyer applied, in imitation of Behrens, for their pre–World War I collaborative work, and the analogies to ancient Egyptian architecture, found in their model factory design for the Werkbund in 1914, are references to this image of the originality that marks the beginnings of a new culture born of industry.[45]

"The powerful physical presence" that Gropius described as the dominant quality of the Dakota elevator in Buffalo was a result of the unbroken surface, even though the middle section of the tall fabric consisted only of thin "arched sheet-metal plates between iron trusses."[46] This building was "especially important" to Gropius because he felt that its artistic urge was so tangible: "Physicality can be composed of any kind of material component and no material, however constituted, will overthrow this basic principle of architecture."[47]

The builders of the American silos seem to "have retained a healthy, whole, and independent natural sense for large, spare form."[48] Gropius held that, in contrast to "overeducated Europeans," they retained an "artistic naiveté." Adolf Behne, influenced by the photographs Gropius had published, also felt that: "the American architect finds himself in much happier circumstances. He isn't hampered by tradition in his pursuit of creative new ideas in industrial building. . . . It is therefore not difficult to understand why America still has the best industrial buildings and why it can be a model for us in this area. Many of our architects have come to the same conclusion. A study tour overseas has become more or less *de rigeur*. Even Peter Behrens went to America last year!"[49]

In Behne's view, the decisive factor was the "uncompromising objectivity of the American approach to industrial tasks." Hence: "the wonderful coal and grain silos and elevators . . . merit the greatest architectural interest, [it doesn't matter] whether they have been designed by artists in our sense of the word or by engineers, [nor] whether their beauty—because of their genesis—is more like the beauty of a machine than the beauty of architecture deliberately conceived as a work of art. What matters is that they are 'beautiful' and that they fall into the domain of architects in our country. And if our architects learn from the American elevators and silos only one thing, namely the extreme minimalism in the use of forms and elements, then the study of those works would already be valuable!"[50]

Prior to World War I, Behne had singled out Poelzig as coming closest to an "uncompromising objectivity," while relegating Gropius to the circle around Behrens's industrial classicism. In the 1920s, he modified this evaluation enough to note the "compromises between object and form, between America and Ostendorf" in the Fagus building: "It is obvious how liberating the study of American industrial buildings has been. What is also obvious is that Gropius nevertheless passes American directness through a quasi-aesthetic filter. . . . The simplicity [of the Fagus building] is actually quite complex. What is more important, however, is that this is the most modern, the prewar German factory building par excellence—maybe not as compellingly simple as Poelzig's . . . but, without a doubt, more daring."[51]

Modern Building Materials: Concrete, Steel, Glass

In 1910, shortly before receiving the commission for the Fagus factory, Gropius told Alma Mahler of his architectural vision: "The most beautiful buildings are those that are built in one's mind but are never executed. I would like to build a large factory entirely of white concrete, all blank walls with large holes in them—large plate-glass panes—and a black roof. A great, pure, richly structured shape, undisturbed by small color variations, painterly values, and architectural curlicues. Impact achieved solely with bright walls and shadows. Simple. Egyptian quietude. Increasingly, I am convinced that work is the only true deity of our time and in art we must help find an expression for it."[52]

His fascination with concrete soon resulted in a commission from the Deutscher Werkbund to author a brochure on the topic.[53] He never seems to have written the brochure, but his comments at the time bear witness to his enthusiasm about two characteristics of the material, which are also typical of the American silos: the bright white-gray hue and the closed surface and fabric formation. In contrast to iron or steel, which are dissolved into framework or girders to save material and to demonstrate the flow of forces, concrete is compressed into compact supports or walls.[54] Gropius understood that "the shaping of volume and—as a necessary consequence—the delimitation of space are the essential task in the art of building." Thanks to its natural qualities, concrete was a building material "predestined for use in monumental design."[55]

In Gropius's early writings, steel and iron are only mentioned in cases where they exude a compact corporality—as in the Dakota Elevator in Buffalo. Peter Behrens had already

chosen plate girders to give more volume to the supports in the longitudinal front of the
Turbine factory. Behrens emphasized "the architectural approach of contracting the iron
volumes instead of dissolving them, as is commonly done in standard grid construction."[56]
To Behrens and his followers, the classic examples of iron architecture—the Crystal Palace
and the Eiffel Tower, for example—were "birdcages" or "bare scaffolds."[57]

For his Hagen lecture, Gropius used a beam bridge to demonstrate how the architect
could "subdue" the dematerializing property of iron in construction. In a photograph, he
blacked in the right-hand section of the bridge "to show how much stronger the architectural impact would be if the builder had used a simple cladding around the lattice.
Instead of a network of innumerable wire rods, he would have achieved, aesthetically
speaking, the impression of a simple, three-dimensional beam and, at the same time, the
eye of any passerby would find better visual purchase."[58] This was to become Gropius's
guiding principle for a long time; well into the 1920s, he continued to set the bridge
example as a task for his architecture students at the Bauhaus in Weimar—much to their
chagrin.[59]

In his pre–World War I texts, Gropius mentioned glass as a building material only in
connection with steel and iron. He did not undertake a more in-depth study of its unique
characteristics. Obviously, glass required the stabilizing solidity of iron, but, like the latter,
it had to be integrated into the overall effect of mass: "Modern building materials such as
iron and glass seem to be incompatible with architecture's need for corporality because
they reveal their inherent insubstantiality. It would be all the more interesting . . . to prove
how the artistic intent can overcome such seemingly insurmountable difficulties, and how,
by sheer craft, it can coax a semblance of solidity from this ethereal material."[60]

Gropius used Behrens's Turbine factory and Poelzig's Werdermühle in Wroclaw
(Silesia) to illustrate how this challenge could be met. In the first building, glass was combined to cover large surfaces and the slant of the windows or the pylons contributed to
shaping a boxy three-dimensionality. Poelzig, on the other hand, went even further by creating independent fabrics that were positioned in front of the main building or that acted
as a bridge between two buildings.[61]

The multistory windows in the main building of the Fagus factory should be read in this manner. Their physical presence is even stronger than in the preliminary design from May 1911, where they were expressed as wide oriels. As I have mentioned earlier, Gropius and Meyer followed examples found in office buildings. The Papierhaus in Berlin, built by Bruno Schmitz in 1906, is one such example; clearly, multistory windows divided only by metal plate parapets between the pylons were already part of the architectural vocabulary of the genre. Even though an antithetical critique of the Turbine factory ultimately influenced how the main building in Alfeld was executed, the comparison to Schmitz illustrates how Gropius and Meyer went beyond Behrens and were also rooted in tactile modern architectural circles in Berlin.

If we read the glazing in the main building as an architectural—that is, spatial and corporeal—use of an ethereal material, then it follows that we should interpret the corner section as a "tactile cube."[62] In its three-dimensionality, the corner presents an ideal situation in which to give volume shape and is much more convincing in its corporality than are the boxy standard fields. The nearly flush joint between coping and glazing contributes to the precise and sharp-edged silhouette, while the battered piers create dark shadows and enhance the depth perspective of the windows. From a passing train, one notices the uniformity of a rhythmically structured facade. Approaching on foot, one begins to differentiate between projecting and receding building components and caesurae. Finally, standing right in front of the building, the eye is drawn to the artfully designed details.[63]

Thus, the building fulfills the "three main phases" in development that, according to Riegl, run through the "visual arts in all ancient cultures of note:" the "tactile" interpreta-

tion of the artistic urge, which emphasizes the contour; the "tactile-optical" conception, which is noticeable above all in the relief-like structure, especially through shadows; the "optical," which emphasizes the individual form in its third dimension. The common basis is given through "awakening the perception of the tactile impenetrability as a condition of material individuality."[64] Or, in Gropius's words, "Independent of the characteristics of the material, architecture must assert the tactile impenetrability of the building components as an indispensable prerequisite for monumental corporality and spatial impact, and overcome the resistance that arises from a particular material."[65]

Transparency as an immaterial quality of glass was another topic that Gropius did not discuss in his writings. Weightlessness, lightness, and the dissolution of the building fabric—the essential characteristics that retrospectively mark the main building in Alfeld as the "seminal building of the international modern style"—did not feature in the architect's theories in 1911. This may explain the perplexing fact that the photographs that document the first construction phase of the Fagus factory did nothing to highlight the main building, or the glass facade, or even the corner without piers. The same can be said of how the Fagus factory was reproduced in pre–World War I publications. The only exception was an advertising brochure for the window manufacturer; here, the reproduction of the main elevation clearly depicts the expanse of glazing, although Gropius never used this photograph in his publications.

The importance we attach to the Fagus factory today was recognized and publicized only in the second half of the 1920s—supported by the contemporary and extensively published series of photographs that featured, above all, the main building and the glass aspect. Its fame as the "seminal building of the international modern style" has little to do with Gropius and Meyer's original intent. This revised interpretation is largely due to Gropius himself, who, from the mid-1920s onward, presented his entire oeuvre as a logical development, beginning with the Fagus factory through to the Werkbund model factory and on to the Bauhaus building itself—proof of overcoming architectural styles of previous centuries and the beginning of modernism in building.

At this time, too, Gropius began "to revisit the idea of space . . . believing that the prevailing perception of space as something enclosed and fully surrounded will give way to a new type of space whose dissolution and lightness will be defined only by individual points of bearing that dictate its rhythm." This new idea of space was expressed in a "feeling of soaring lightness."[66] From this point forward, Gropius would connect lightness with the characteristics of glass, iron, and concrete as building materials. Thus, by 1926, he arrived at a view diametrically opposed to the one he had held in 1911. He maintained that "the principle of movement, the traffic of our time, is reflected in relieving the building fabric and the rooms, rejecting the wall as an endpoint and seeking the connection between interior space and universal space. These buildings express weightlessness, lightness, a rhythmic animation; gravity, the earth's inertia are overcome in impression and appearance."[67]

In 1911, however, the intention had not been to show limitless space but to contain it. The transparency of glass was not used to produce dissolution or a flowing transition between interior and exterior. As Gropius rarely expressed opinions on glass as a building material prior to World War I, our only recourse is to look at his other buildings of the same period to try to understand the importance, if any, of glass as a building material.

Aside from factory construction, glass was commonly used by Gropius and Meyer in winter gardens and greenhouses. It is also a feature in the design for the new Alfeld hospital in 1912; the operating theatre is marked by the floor-height windows set in box frames projecting from the wall that were repeated in the projected design for the addition to the tool-and-die shop at the Fagus factory in 1914. Glass was not employed to lay bare the activities that took place inside but to optimize light conditions. Yet, even the light conditions were not the main reason behind the design, as the greenery hanging from the roof garden demonstrates. Instead, the glass cladding was intended to draw attention to the special function of this wing: an ultramodern, hygienic workplace where science and technology were put in the service of health care.

The same criteria applied to the outstanding operation and management of the Fagus factory: Benscheidt Sr.'s motto was *progress*, especially with regard to optimized work conditions, modern factory equipment, and the reformist goal of healthy footwear. "Brightness, orderliness, and cleanliness" had already been praised as the main features of the production rooms in the Behrens Shoe Last factory. Now the Fagus factory was to "declare even by its exterior what a modern workplace it is."[68] The ethereal quality of glass

Alfeld hospital. Design by Walter Gropius and Adolf Meyer, 1912.

may well make it the most appropriate building material to express immaterial qualities such as "light, air, and purity" while satisfying the "great communal ideal"[69] that Gropius wished to provide for the workers in accordance with Benscheidt Sr.'s principles.

The use of glass, however, does not automatically translate into transparency in the sense of an open presentation of translucency. The few areas where it was nevertheless demonstratively applied were those that had a representative or public character—during the first building phase, for example, on the office floor, where the glass partitions allowed visitors a view into the ultramodern administration offices. In this instance, the transparency of the material was meant to suggest a similar transparency—read openness—in the business operations. During the second construction phase, in 1913–1914, the glazed south corner exposed the stairs and guided visitors to the offices. Finally, one should mention the power house as a glass cube designed to display the generator—the heart of the complex—following a tradition in factory architecture.

The curtain glazing in the Fagus factory created good light conditions even in the farthest corners of each room; but the abundance of light also presented unforeseen problems. From the outset, curtains were used in each room of the main building. Even in the production hall, the relatively small windows installed during the first construction phase were covered with blinds, as we can see in photographs taken in 1912. After the extension was built in 1913–1914 and the southwest section was fully glazed, the bottom panels of each row of windows were covered in opaque paint. Obviously, the northeast light that penetrated from the glazed sawtooth roof was more than adequate and provided a better and more evenly distributed light. Awnings were installed after 1926 on the street facade of the production hall and only then was the opaque paint removed from the windowpanes.

Nevertheless, the architects continued to employ glass as a building material and, together with the trussless corner, glazing is the architectural trademark of the Fagus factory, adaptations of which were also used for the smaller buildings and projects that followed in the 1920s. This distinctive feature—and its reprisal in the Bauhaus building in 1925–1926—has inspired serious critical commentary as well as polemic comparisons to departmet-store architecture.[70] However, as a building material, glass was not merely employed to display commercial goods. It also emerged from architectural trends in factory and office buildings.

The high real-estate prices and deep lots in the cities of late nineteenth century were the key factors behind an increased use of large windowpanes. Like the factory floors in courtyard buildings in Berlin, the rear offices in Liverpool, Glasgow, and Chicago were commercially viable only if they provided good natural light. This had less to do with pretensions to providing humane working conditions than with the cost of electricity, which was especially high in rural areas. During the period when the Fagus factory was operating in a temporary setup (1910–1911), Benscheidt Sr. paid "0.25 marks per kilowatt hour of artificial light,"[71] an amount his American partners found exorbitantly high.

Since the turn of the century, large-span halls and workshop buildings in steel or concrete construction with expansive glazing had become more popular. The illustrations Gropius used for Gropius's lecture at Hagen were a case in point. In America, daylight factories, whose very name underscored the advantages of natural light, were examples of a new type of building in factory architecture. Gropius included photographs of such buildings in the collection on excellence in industrial building. Surprisingly, the factory complex of the United Shoe Machinery Corporation in Beverly, Massachusetts (1903–1905), was not among them, although that company had been the financial backer that enabled the foundation of Fagus GmbH in the first place. For its time, the United Shoe complex was the largest concrete factory building and was considered the best of its kind in all aspects.[72] As I have mentioned before, Benscheidt Jr. worked in this factory for a short period in 1911 to familiarize himself with the American approach to works management.

But the sober architecture created by Ernest Ransome, the American engineer, and Gropius and Meyer's work, rooted as it was in a profound theory, have little in common. Similarly constructed workshop complexes, albeit less advanced from the perspective of building technology, were quite well-known in Germany at the time. They belonged to a category of buildings that the architecture critic Karl Scheffler called "glass barns."[73] The critic would probably have attached the same label to the Steiff factory, built a few years earlier in Giengen on the Brenz. The location of the complex was as provincial as that of Fagus, and it too remained relatively unknown, while its products—the famous stuffed animals with the buttoned earlobes—are a household name to German children even today.

In the years after 1903, several fully glazed multistory factory buildings were constructed on the site in Giengen. On the exterior, the double-layered glass skin rose from the ground to the top floor, turning the corners around supports that had been realized as a frame. On the interior, the glass skin reached from floor to ceiling—that is, a single story. The steel structure stood between the two layers of glass. The subsequent buildings were erected with a nail-holding wood construction that was easier to realize on site. The Steiff buildings are still a good example of a sophisticated yet pragmatic use of glass in early twentieth-century architecture. The unassuming utilitarian building (surely more functional than the Fagus factory, because its double skin and matte glass in the internal layer resulted in better thermal and light conditions) was radical in a rational, unselfconscious manner; clearly, this was the work of an engineer, not an architect/artist. Here, too, glass was used not only for its transparency but also because it communicated modernity. This

United Shoe Machinery Corporation, Beverly, Massachusetts, near Boston. Design by Ernest L. Ransome, 1903–1905.

comes across in a photograph from the early 1920s in which three generations of transportation stand in front of the buildings marked with the year of their construction: horse-drawn wagon, electric trolley, and car. Similar photographs were taken in Alfeld in 1924 against the backdrop of the main building (see photo on page 111).

The client and the architects were more ambitious in their demands for the Fagus factory. Both wanted the building to mark a new phase in their professional careers while setting new standards in the field—establishing a prototype, as it were. The goal was to create an example for a new monumental style derived from industrial architecture: dignity, advertising, and modernity expressed in an artistically stylized factory as an embodiment of industrial culture. Glass was the primary means of expressing this goal. As illustrated in an advertising flyer for glass building blocks from the late 1930s, the Fagus factory and glass were not only present in the minds of architectural historians but also in those of advertising executives.

"Each material," Gropius wrote in 1911, "finds its master."[74] In the case of glass, the master would be Walter Gropius.

Advertisement for Siemens
Glas AG, circa 1939.

Fagus and the Bauhaus

Karl Benscheidt Jr. (1888–1975)

While Carl Benscheidt Sr. had been the driving force behind founding the Fagus factory and managing it during World War I, after 1919, his son stepped into the foreground. On a management level, this generational shift expressed itself in a switch from GmbH (limited liability company) to trading company, with father and son as sole proprietors; the new company, officially introduced on April 30, 1919, carried the name of the junior director, "Fagus-Werk Karl Benscheidt."

These changes were precipitated by the events of World War I. A small percentage of the capital invested in the Fagus GmbH came from England. When war broke out, the company was first put under government supervision and then, when the

Karl Benscheidt Jr. Factory photo, circa 1930.

United States entered the war in 1917, it went into receivership. Benscheidt Sr. correctly anticipated a forced liquidation and—after consulting with his American partners—was able to prevent this by initiating a liquidation himself; with the help of a bank loan he then promptly bought the company back from the German state.

Benscheidt Sr. proved to be an exceptionally quick-minded and sure-handed businessman, and not only in this matter. It was due to his experience, his ability to improvise, and his vision that Fagus survived the war years with balanced books. Shoes were an essential war product and were manufactured only for the military. Hence, production of footwear for civilians came to a halt and with it the production of shoes that changed with the fashion. This meant that the demand for shoe lasts dropped to almost nil. The Fagus factory

Opposite: Main office in new addition. Photo by Edmund Lill, first half of 1923.

quickly switched to manufacturing all kinds of secondary products, such as clogs, wood soles, and wood nails.

Being the good entrepreneur that he was, Benscheidt Sr. knew that the demand for shoes would soar after the war. He prepared for the postwar era by investing in raw material. Thus, the Fagus factory had a large stock of rough lasts by 1918, accumulated through advantageous purchases of wood. The lasts required a long drying process anyway and could be stored until they were needed. By 1920, Benscheidt Sr. could write to his American friends, with whom he had maintained good business relations, that he was "able to show them a factory, which surely deserves to be called exemplary with regard to equipment, stock, organization, etc."[1]

In the immediate aftermath of the war, Benscheidt Sr. earned profits that he invested in property and real estate during the currency devaluation of 1922–1923. In this manner, he was able to acquire adjacent companies and undeveloped sites, which enabled him to increase the size of his own factory site on two sides. Some of these purchased buildings were used for production while others were renovated into workers' housing. The upswing was short-lived, however, for in 1926 a massive currency turnover of 40 percent sparked a regressive trend that would last well beyond the depression of 1929. For the shoe industry, the reason for the omnipresent recession lay in the increasing rationalization that was being implemented in factories everywhere.[2] While Benscheidt continued to stick to the principle of quality and sought expansion through export trade, his competitors responded to the recession with cheap goods and discounts as low as 25 percent, which meant the ruin of this industry sector. Of some twenty shoe-last factories in Germany, only nine survived this period; of these, Fagus was the second largest.

The company survived these difficult years only because of its innovative approach. After World War I, it no longer specialized in a few products; instead, the focus shifted to

Fagus ironing tools. Photo by Albert Renger-Patzsch, April 1928. Fagus series no. 42.

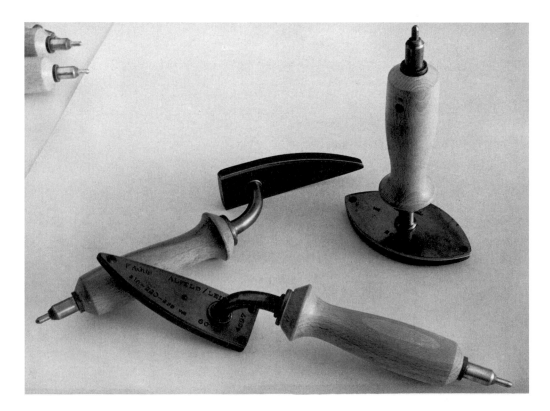

developing new products and optimizing production. Father and son Benscheidt adroitly spotted any niche in the market. A brief notice in a trade journal, for instance, lamenting the poor quality of standard ironing tools, inspired them to bring improved electric models onto the market. Albert Renger-Patzsch's photographs of this simple tool, used to iron out the seams resulting from mechanical shoe production, eventually made them famous. The irons are still produced today in almost the same fashion.

The Fagus precision lathe was developed by Benscheidt Jr. after years of study. The lathe could reproduce irregular shapes in wood so accurately that even a stamp could be recognizably transferred. In shoe-last production, this machine eliminated the need for several finishing steps; it maintained and protected the integrity of the model and was able to turn right and left lasts without distortion. Furthermore, it could be upgraded to a double lathe and still require only one operator. While the machine had originally been improved for in-house purposes, by the late 1920s Fagus began not only to build the machine but also to export it—above all, to other European countries that did not import shoe lasts from Fagus.

The unusual performance of this lathe soon attracted attention and, in 1925, the editor of *Das Kunstblatt* was prompted to exclaim after a visit to the factory: "Wouldn't it be strange if someone had the idea of strapping a small sculpture by Riemenschneider or the Egyptian figurine of a water carrier from the Louvre collection into one of these machines and then carve duplicates by the thousands? It could easily be done and the copy—for the machine cannot falsely reproduce—would be devoid of the small inconsistencies inherent to human efforts at copying originals."[3] In later years, Benscheidt Jr. would repeat this tale to visitors—rounding out the anecdotal character of this performance test with a smile.

Fagus precision lathe. Factory photo, 1930s.

Benscheidt Jr.'s area of responsibility included the construction office, the mechanical engineering department, and the electric workshop. Years of practice had prepared him well for this task. With regard to his son's training, Benscheidt Sr. had "always envisioned that he would one day either join a business where I was manager or take over a company that I had established."[4] So after his son graduated, Benscheidt sent him to apprentice in a shoe factory, where he learned all aspects of shoe production and the business aspects of the trade from the bottom up. Following his apprenticeship, Benscheidt Jr. attended the renowned Berlin School of Business and Trade for two semesters and then spent the year of 1910–1911 working in American factories.

Several factory notebooks from his time in America, filled with notes on production processes and details of mechanical engineering, tell of his strong interest in all technical installations that he perceived to be new and useful. Notes on impractical installations or processes were always accompanied by suggestions and ideas for improvement. Easing the workload and improving function were uppermost in his mind. These notebooks also contain entries that indicate that he may have known Frederick Winslow Taylor's time studies.[5]

The primary sources give us an insight into the works organization of the Fagus factory from 1920 onward only. It is nearly impossible to deduce whether or not any of the methods were specifically American. At Fagus, the practice seems to have been to integrate a variety of ideas that were compatible with the specific requirements of last production. One of these was to abolish the old foreman system. Specially equipped control stations, set up along the production path and manned by workers, took over the supervisory role and ensured that errors were caught early.[6] The foreman was replaced, by 1924 at the latest, by a factory engineer whose office was separated from the production hall by a glass partition and slightly raised to provide a better view of what was going on.

In a lecture in 1927, Benscheidt Jr. elaborated on the methods employed by American car manufacturer Henry Ford, whom he must have met during his stay.[7] In contrast to the focus on a single mass-produced model, as in the case of Ford, shoe lasts were a specialized product for which orders arrived for a specific number of pieces. Ford's practices were therefore not applicable to Fagus. The only storage possibilities were those of the rough lasts. Actual last production could begin only when an order came in, each time with the need to consider specific client wishes. "Therefore, we cannot speak here of modern mass production, but we can speak of a highly modernized artisan's workshop or artisan's trade."[8] In contrast to America, "the land of mass production of cheap consumer goods," Benscheidt Jr. thought of the Fagus factory as a symbol of work methods in Germany— "the ideal country for meeting individual client demands."

At Fagus, the factory engineer was responsible for constantly modernizing the operation. Beyond the actual production area, he initiated optimization measures in all departments: keeping an index-card record of the clientele and the raw material inventory, issuing inventory numbers for every single object in the factory, installing measuring devices on nearly all machines and uniform locks on all doors, strictly adhering to the German Industrial Standards format (or DIN)—to mention just a few of the engineer's responsibilities. Although the urge to optimize and organize tended to take over at times, overall it benefited not only production efficacy but also safety at the workplace. The Fagus factory had the lowest accident rate in the industry. Refunded insurance premiums flowed directly into the company's health insurance fund.

Training received special emphasis. Workers were expected to master the entire production process, from raw material to finished product—on the one hand, to prevent alienation from work, and, on the other hand, to be ready to step in wherever they were needed. This strategy proved very successful, especially for rationalization measures—for example, when the precision lathe came into operation. Apprentices for the position of last model maker were selected on the basis of psychological aptitude tests.[9] Each day ended with an additional hour of instruction in the works school, founded in 1927, and the junior director also gave lessons. The in-house library offered material for adult education; there were technical books on last production and mechanical engineering, a belles lettres section, and material on the artistic avant-garde, such as a series of Bauhaus books.

The titles are a reflection of Karl Benscheidt Jr.'s wide range of interests; he turned out to be less the rational engineer than an aesthete with a keen feeling for the arts. Walter Gropius opened the doors to modern art and architecture and we find that the junior director was involved in all the activities and groups in which Gropius participated, such as the Arbeitsrat für Kunst (Workers' Council for the Arts), whose manifesto he signed in 1919.[10] Father and son Benscheidt were faithful supporters of the Bauhaus through commissions, product purchases, and even specific donations and interest-free loans.

The model home Am Horn in Weimar was one of the projects they supported; in two installments in March and April 1923, the Benscheidts contributed a dizzying sum of 1.5 million marks (inflated, naturally, because of the concurrent currency devaluation). In early September 1924, they advanced 4,000 marks to Gropius to help him reorganize his practice, which was being integrated into the architecture department at the Bauhaus.[11] When the government of Thuringia canceled the Bauhaus contracts at the end of 1924, Gropius attempted to transform it into a limited liability company. Again, the junior director helped out by authorizing a 3,000-mark deposit.[12] In the end, after the Bauhaus moved from Weimar to Dessau, both father and son officially joined the circle of Friends of the Bauhaus.

In 1922, inspired by the pathos of expressionism, Benscheidt Jr. founded the Volksbildungverein (Association for Public Adult Education) together with four other supporters in Alfeld. The founding manifesto, a three-page proclamation, enthusiastically juxtaposed progress in technology, scientific innovation, and artistic expression with the "pure materialism" of the prewar era. Similar to the Bauhaus manifesto (1919), this pamphlet proclaimed that "Building encompasses all arts. From buildings we can learn more about how different peoples feel and think than from many history books. Show me the architecture of an era and I'll tell you how people lived and thought."[13]

The goal of the association was to "invite men of the arts and sciences who have seen the land of the future to tell us of the miracles they have seen." Walter Gropius accepted the invitation to hold the first lecture and delivered a presentation on the Bauhaus. Announcing the event, Benscheidt Jr. introduced Gropius as follows: "He works to counteract the separation of art disciplines by gathering them all into architecture. While this goal has been attempted for centuries, it has never been attained. In three years, Gropius has proven that he has, despite the difficulties and struggles that inevitably confront such an endeavor, especially in our time."[14]

As Benscheidt Jr. had identified the Fagus factory as an example of Gropius's radical sense of building, it seemed logical to present it as an embodiment of the "Gesamtkunstwerk" that everyone was striving for. One should remember that the interior of the main building was designed in collaboration with Bauhaus artists and craftsmen during this same period in 1922–1923. Yet this was a reciprocal relationship; the Bauhaus, too, presented its collaboration with the Fagus factory as a fulfillment of its mission, expressed in its latest motto in 1923 as "Art and Technology—a New Unity." For the exhibition *Die Form* in Stuttgart in 1924, the Bauhaus planned a special presentation with the Fagus factory that comprised photographs of the architecture and also introduced "shoe lasts, measuring instruments, small appliances for shoe factories and printed matter. . . . These are merely ideas that inspire the owner to show how thoroughly the idea of form has been translated into reality, from factory building to product."[15] The "small appliances" probably included the ironing tool and the corresponding wall socket, both designed by Gropius.[16] The Fagus factory embodied both Bauhaus ideals: the "big building" of the Gesamtkunstwerk and artist collaboration in designing industrial products.

Benscheidt Jr., who frequently went to Erfurt on business, seems to have attended nearly all functions at the Bauhaus in Weimar; the guest list for the festive inauguration of the new Bauhaus at Dessau in December 1926 included Benscheidt Sr. and Jr. Furthermore, the junior director maintained close contacts with other Bauhaus artists such as Werner Gilles, Laszlo Moholy-Nagy, Karl Peter Röhl, and Eberhard Schrammen—that is, not only with the masters but also with Bauhaus students. The latter were all close friends of Adolf Meyer.

In the summer of 1925, the Benscheidts prepared for a trip to Holland. Meyer provided them with a list of new architecture they should visit and with the addresses of all the artists in the Dutch group De Stijl; with such preparation, their vacation turned into an informative tour of the modern movement. W.M. Dudok, C. v. Eesteren, J.J.P. Oud, and G. Rietveld were all available to give advice and information and, in some instances, act as personal guides through their buildings. Thus not only the name of Benscheidt but also the Fagus factory itself became known to the Dutch scene.

But Benscheidt Jr. didn't limit his contacts to the Bauhaus and Bauhaus artists; he was also an active supporter of the modern movement in Hanover. He joined the Kestnergesellschaft and was a founding member of the association known as die abstrakten hanover (the abstract artists of Hanover) in 1927.[17] It must have been there, or possibly through his acquaintances, which included Karl Buchheister, El Lissitzky, Kurt Schwitters, and Friedrich Vordemberge-Gildewart, that he met the American gallery owner Katherine Dreier.[18] He usually invited new artists he met to Alfeld for a tour of the Fagus factory; after the mid-1920s, the factory's gate was like a revolving door for artists from the international avant-garde.[19]

Benscheidt Jr. turned to reading whenever he was unable to experience something he was interested in first-hand; as a member of the Werkbund, he subscribed to *Die Form*, and, as a Friend of the Bauhaus, he received the magazine *Bauhaus-Zeitschrift*; in addition, he read *G-Zeitschrift für elementare Gestaltung* and his personal library contained issues of *Neues Russland* as well as *Esprit Nouveau*.[20] Furthermore, Benscheidt Jr. was one of the few subscribers to the Dutch *De Stijl* magazine in Germany. All this makes it amply clear that he was as familiar with international trends in the arts and in architecture as were his architects.

The younger Benscheidt was also a great supporter of science. Like his father before him, he studied how lasts could be improved to create more foot-friendly shoes. He gathered his findings in tables that listed last sizes in exact measurements for both width and length; he also developed customized equipment, such as a device to standardize heel measurements and a measuring-point marker for greater precision in last production, again in the interest of improving the fit of shoes. All these efforts were, however, only small steps toward the ultimate goal of an absolute reform in the way shoes were manufactured in mass production. To this end, however, basic medical research was still inadequate.

In 1921, Benscheidt Jr. met Dr. August Weinert, an orthopedic specialist who had dedicated his life to the scientific study of the human foot. Fagus provided generous financial and practical support for his research for over a decade. Weinert's greatest achievements were the definition of the "normal" or average foot and the analysis of foot movements in walking. He maintained that natural movement would place the foot in the so-called optimal position. The foot, it turned out, is a torsion; while the posterior section of the foot turns outward (supination-varus position), the anterior section of the foot rotates inward (pronation-valgus position).[21]

Yet Weinert had difficulty in proving that people's feet took on this "optimal position"; he discovered examples only among native peoples, athletes, and statues from antiquity. The foot of (so-called) civilized man was invariably deformed from wearing badly fitting shoes. The main culprit was the usual shape of lasts, which traced the human foot in the wide-spread but deformed valgus position. Weinert succeeded in returning his patients' feet to the optimal position through massage and exercises, and by educating patients about proper footwear.

In collaboration with Benscheidt Jr., Weinert began to develop an anatomically correct shoe last. Together with a master shoemaker named Siebert, who held several patents on lasts in a varus position of the posterior foot and for various shoe manufacturers, they founded the Angulus Varus Company in 1926. The goal of the organization was to manufacture healthy yet fashionable footwear for men, women, and children. The shoe would place the posterior foot at the correct angle to the leg axis—that is, into the varus position (hence the name of the organization, from Latin: *angulus*, or angle, and *varus*).

Father and son Benscheidt set great store by this endeavor because it had more in com-

Left to right: skeleton of "normal" foot; skeleton of slightly deformed foot; skeleton of "medium" flat foot. Photos by Albert Renger-Patzsch, 1926.

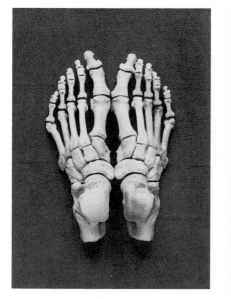
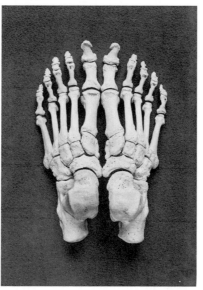
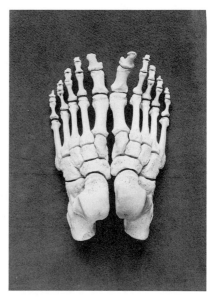

Scenes from Angulus Varus film; consultation in shoe boutique. Photos by Albert Renger-Patzsch, circa 1928.

mon with their goal of producing quality "reform" goods than any other previous Fagus product. At the same time, it opened possibilities for diversification just when sales for their main product were dropping. From the beginning, they understood that shoes manufactured from Varus lasts would sell only if they were also elegant. This was not to be a "sensible health shoe" for the minority who were, at any rate, already converted to the need for such footwear. Instead, mass impact was the goal—to ensure sales, naturally, but also because the Benscheidts had a genuine desire to improve the health of the population at large. Finally, these experimental contracts were an excellent opportunity to test the Fagus precision lathe.

In 1927–1928, Weinert launched the Angulus Varus shoe with an intensive advertising campaign. Johannes Molzahn designed the poster, several product brochures, and the shoeboxes. He incorporated photographs by Albert Renger-Patzsch, who had begun taking the pictures a year earlier in 1926, enabling Weinert to use the prints for his own work and to illustrate a scientific essay.[22] The pictures are of shoes, feet, and foot skeletons deformed from wearing ill-fitting shoes. The daylight shots of the skeletons against a black background were especially challenging, from a technical perspective.[23] Despite this, Renger-Patzsch seems not to have thought highly of them because they are not listed in his subsequent catalog.[24]

There was even a demonstration film entitled *Die Bedeutung richtiger Fußbekleidung für die Volksgesundheit* (*The Importance of Correct Footwear for Public Health*). All that remains are a few stills, presumably by Renger-Patzsch, which were incorporated into a brochure.[25] Ultimately, however, we cannot prove that these are, in fact, stills from a film possibly even directed by Renger-Patzsch; the brochure may simply have been designed to simulate a cinematic scenario. The scene is a shoe store, where two women customers and a salesperson are engaged in conversation; the saleswoman is explaining the advantages of the Angulus Varus shoe.[26]

The partners in the Angulus Varus GmbH disagreed on many fundamental issues and by 1928 the difficulties seemed insurmountable. When Weinert was forced to concede that the Angulus Varus shoe forced the foot into an unhealthy motion, the partnership with the manufacturers broke up for good.

Combining science and art and transforming the combination into a "reform" product was a costly and idealistic risk that was doomed to fail because the scientific basis simply

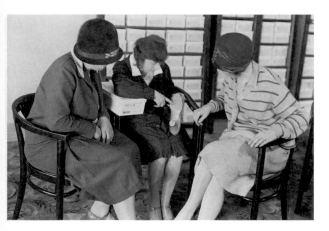

did not yet exist. But the Angulus Varus did have one positive outcome for the public: shoes with the uncomfortable pes valgus shape (club-foot position) disappeared from the market altogether.

Smaller Projects after 1919

Immediately after the end of the war, Gropius reestablished contact with the Benscheidts. By mid-January 1919, he was once again in Alfeld to inspect the buildings that had been completed while he was at the front. This was a period for small projects, such as the upright clock that Gropius and Meyer designed after they resumed their joint practice in March 1919; rather conventional manner, it was specified in the drawings as "standard clock, production hall." In September of the same they redesigned the lettering on the roof of the warehouse, necessary because of the official change to the company name.

During these months, too, Gropius and Meyer worked at supervising the completion of the boiler and power houses. The railing in front of the building—standard gas tubes with spherical connectors and spiral finials—was also begun in 1919, but the interior of the power house was completed only by the end of 1922. The finishing touch in the strictly black-and-white décor of the room was a black painted line: at level with the upper edge of the window frame, it continued on the adjacent wall and ended on either side of the central clock face on the front wall. Similar graphic wall decorations in the vestibule, completed at the same time, identify this rather plain attribute in the machine house as a decorative element. The furniture—a long table and at least two of the chairs—was probably also based on designs by Gropius and Meyer; one chair, originally painted in the characteristic turquoise but now covered in white, still exists.

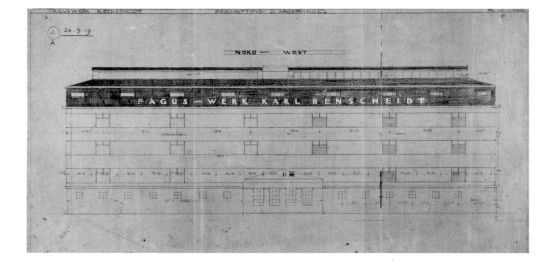

New lettering on warehouse, 1919.

This postwar period is sparsely documented, but a design for a display cabinet is dated May 1921. The wide but shallow cabinet had a low base divided into three sections and a tall glass top. With its beveling and short, pyramid legs, it is a typical example of the expressionistic furniture designed by Gropius and Meyer. Together with the bookcases for the ladies' salon in Berlin's Villa Sommerfeld (1921–1922) and for the study in the Hanstein apartment in Homberg-Efze (1923–1924), this display case for the Fagus factory should be seen as the prototype for subsequent pieces.[27]

Interior Design and Furniture for the Main Building, 1921–1925

The outbreak of World War I had left the extension to the main building unfinished on the inside. The shipping department was set up on the ground floor as planned, but the two upper floors were utilized for production during the war years. Drawings for the interior design of the vestibule had been finished by July 1914. In 1921–1922, the design was finally executed, with little modification to the original drawings.

Here too, Gropius and Meyer employed black glass to divide the white walls into sections, as they had done in the office building for the Werkbund model factory in Cologne in 1914. The contrast of positive and negative shapes was a new interpretation of antique ornamental styles.[28] The wall design with a base, linear ornamentation, and, above all, the frieze, complete with metope and triglyphs, echoed the formal language of antiquity. These elements all contributed to the ceremonial mood, creating the awe-inspiring effect that monumental architecture was to have on visitors and to which Gropius subscribed in his pre–World War I work.

The decision to execute a design that was, after all, seven years old was surely more than a matter of convenience or of catering to the client's desire. The design was simply good

Power house. Photo by Edmund Lill, November 1922.

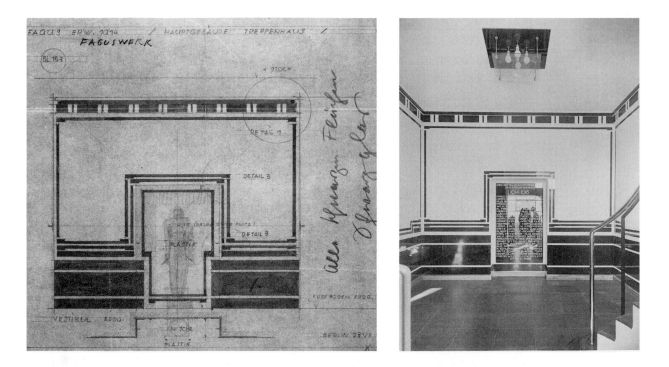

Vestibule in main building.
Left: Design from 1914.
Right: Completion in 1922. Photo by Edmund Lill, first half of 1923.

and it offered a solid solution. In 1923, Gropius and Meyer created a very similar vestibule for another client, the Spiegelglas AG in nearby Freden. The return to a timeless classicism also characterized other projects they carried out in 1922–1923.

The original plan from 1914 envisioned the placement of a life-size sculpture of a male nude—possibly a work to be commissioned from Richard Scheibe, Gerhard Marcks, and Georg Kolbe—all artists whose pieces Gropius and Meyer had already often integrated into their architecture. In the end, when the vestibule was finally completed in 1922, the sculpture was exchanged for a memorial plaque bearing the names of Fagus employees who had died in World War I. A new angular font, popular at the Bauhaus at that time, was used for the typography.[29]

The lighting fixture for the vestibule ceiling was designed in 1922. It had four bulbs in exposed settings and was attached to the ceiling with a square plate in black glass from which a clear glass plate was suspended by rods; die-shaped nuts attached the clear plate to the rod ends. Recent restoration efforts in the vestibule and the stairwell of the main building have revealed that the fine, white wall finish was interspersed with bits of mica. The glossy glass particles created glittering reflections of light. The inner door panel was originally painted sienna.[30]

The entrance door was also based on a design from Gropius's office. Photographs show that a temporary door covered the opening for the first years. The finished door was made after a drawing that arrived at the factory in January 1922, in which the external door panel is sketched with three parallel lines of nail-heads meandering at a right angle. Similar models are found in the work of the Dutch architect J.L.M. Lauweriks, Adolf Meyer's teacher at the Arts and Crafts School in Düsseldorf.

And last, but not least, there was the door handle. It was a special edition of the famous Gropius handle: a square bar bent at a right angle, with a cylindrical grip. But the design sketch for the vestibule door from January 1922 did not feature this particular handle. Instead, it showed a handle similar to a model designed by Peter Behrens. The Gropius han-

Main entrance door.
Design, 1921–1922.

Handle on main door,
1922.

dle can therefore have been installed only in the course of 1922.[31] Although other sources have attributed the date 1914, this is surely a mistake and is not corroborated by the facts.[32]

The offices on the second floor were expanded during the same period. Again, the vestibule walls were finished in a light-colored plaster containing particles of mica, while the ceiling was covered in a strong cobalt blue. Here stood a three-piece suite consisting of a plain wooden bench, two matching arm chairs, and a square table; the drawings date from March 1925 and indicate that the furniture pieces were to be executed in oak (later painted white). Once again, several authors have erroneously given the date as early as 1910.[33]

The office wing on the railroad side, built in 1911, served as a model for the floor plan. The individual offices lay off a long corridor that ran parallel to the rear wall. From the vestibule, visitors stepped into a square anteroom with a doorway on one side, leading to the conference room, and double swing doors, on the other side, leading into the corridor. A

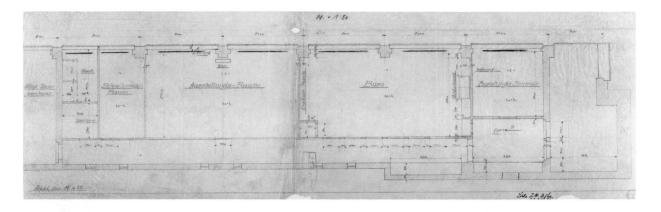

sliding glass window communicated with the adjacent accounting and cashier's office. The anteroom was furnished with a white wooden bench that still exists; it was covered in loose black seat cushions and featured the characteristic beveled edges. The drawing, made in Gropius's office, dates from May 30, 1922.

Around 1922–1923, Bauhaus apprentice Erich Brendel designed a round oak table with six plank-shaped table legs and a tabletop with a star-patterned veneer for the conference room. Six padded armchairs with leather-covered seats and backrests stood around the table. Brendel produced only the prototypes in the Bauhaus carpentry workshop—that is, one chair and the table.[34] The remaining pieces were most likely made in the shop of an Alfeld carpenter. An armchair covered in a striped fabric from the Bauhaus weaving workshop remained in Brendel's possession and was featured in the Bauhaus exhibition of 1923.[35] A second, smaller table, nearly identical to the conference table, together with four

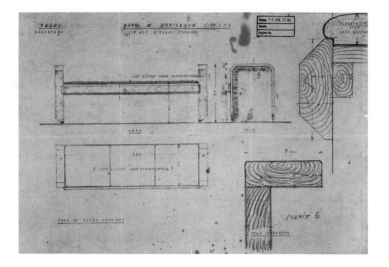

additional armchairs, was donated by Fagus to the Bauhaus collection in Dessau.

As in the main building section on the railroad side, the addition featured a large office space separated from the corridor by a glass partition. The interior featured louvered reed curtains, radiator covers in colored plate glass, a phone booth built into one of the corners, and, naturally, the latest in office furnishings. The door handles, made with a conical grip, were precursors to the Gropius handle. Again, I must emphasize that it is entirely unreasonable to assign a date as early as 1914 to these items.[36] Drawings for office wall sections with a handle identifiable as the Gropius handle are dated July and August 1922. The exact date of completion is not documented. We may, however, safely assume that the space was first occupied in or after the spring of 1923.

Archival material provides no information as to the colors chosen for the interior walls. Only the main stairwell has been restored and research material is therefore still sparse. Black-and-white photographs taken shortly after the completion of the office floor show that the walls in the anteroom were uniformly painted in what appears as a dark tone. The corridor featured a differentiated color scheme with light pillars and, in between, darker parapets and door and window frames. This original color scheme probably remained unchanged well into the 1950s. Unfortunately, the notes and comments that exist are fairly general—for example, "the walls are always kept in a matte green, light yellow, and English red."[37]

Nevertheless, these comments are corroborated by a floor plan for the third floor of the addition. The upper right-hand corner of the drawing contains watercolor samples with detailed notes. According to this sketch, the walls and ceilings were to be painted in blue-green, pillars and girders in light yellow, doors and radiators in gray, and the window frames including muntins and mullions in a reddish purple. This last color choice was common in Gropius and Meyer's designs at that time, although they tended to use it on the exterior—as they did, for example, on the window frames of a storehouse for the Kappe company, built after 1923.[38] The vestibule ceiling on the third floor was also painted red; this is confirmed in a photograph from 1923, where the dark hue in the ceiling is clearly different from the wall color.

Several contemporary sources indicate that the Bauhaus directed the color scheme for the office floor in the main building. Emphasis was put on the "simple, practical approach of the Weimar Bauhaus. . . . It underscores the room architecture with divided surfaces and color selection. This has brought an unexpected freshness and liveliness into the rooms, which cannot but have a positive influence on those working in them."[39] No individual names are given, however, in keeping with the prevalent idea at the time of a joint collaboration to create the Great Building. At the same time, Benscheidt Jr.'s expenses for February 1922 list a visit by "Schlemmer-Weimar" at the end of the month.[40] The visitor may have been either Oskar Schlemmer or Carl Schlemmer, the famous painter's brother, who also worked at the Bauhaus as a shop master. A visit at this period would surely have been for the purpose of gathering information on site only, if it can be seen in the context of a color scheme for the stairwell and the office floor at all.

As soon as the new office floor was completed, the main building's older section on the railroad side was also renovated. The dates on drawings from Gropius's office range

Main building, new office floor. Karl Benscheidt Jr. is standing and speaking on the phone. Photo by Edmund Lill, first half of 1923.

Stairwell in main building, 3rd floor. Photo by Edmund Lill, first half of 1923.

from September 1923 to December 1924 and include even such small details such as a footmat. Considering the relatively small scope of the task in terms of actual constructional changes, the renovation took quite a long time. Only a few of the 5-centimeter partition walls were taken down and moved to accommodate the new use of the space. As the sample room and the cashier were now housed in the new office wing, space for these functions was no longer required in the older section of the building, opening a larger executive office for the senior manager and additional space for a filing department in the main office.

The renovation work was kept to a minimum, no doubt because of the currency devaluation in 1923. The corridor wall was left virtually untouched; only the volutes above the door lintels were removed—obviously, these pseudo-antique decorative details from the prewar years were now considered superfluous. In other words, the wall openings and the doors were left just as they had been. A glass partition was recycled for use in another location. Instead of an upholstered set for the executive office, shown in the floor plan from December 10, 1923, and quite similar to Gropius's own executive suite at the Bauhaus in Weimar, Benscheidt Sr. made do with the plain wicker furniture from 1912.

Beginning in late March 1924, Bauhaus student Peter Keler spent several weeks in Alfeld to paint the office floor.[41] There are no documents that provide information about the original wall color. With the exception of a single photograph by Renger-Patzsch, taken in 1928 as part of the Fagus series, the renovated office floor was never photographed. This one photograph proves, however, that no Gropius handles were installed on the old doors in 1923–1924. The handles, which are in place today, can only have been installed after 1970.[42]

Company Housing:
The Building "Am Weidenknick," 1923

On a property near the factory, purchased by Benscheidt Sr. shortly after World War I, a six-family residential house was built after May 1922, based on plans by architect W. Rudolph from Einbeck. It consisted of three-room apartments for Fagus employees, with a stable and garden plot for each unit. Bruno Hans, employed as an interpreter for foreign trade with Russia, moved into the ground-floor apartment on the right-hand side. Bruno Hans had been an officer before the revolution. He had fled to Germany, where he arrived with only the clothes on his back. The Benscheidts furnished the entire apartment for him.

They commissioned Ernst Neufert to design the furniture and Hinnerk Scheper to conceive the interior color scheme. Although both had left the Bauhaus by this time, the interior was described as a Bauhaus project.[43]

Ernst Neufert (1900–1986) had been a Bauhaus student for a short period in 1919–1920 and was employed as site manager by Gropius in 1922. In 1923, he moved to Alfeld for approximately one year to oversee work on the Fagus factory and some smaller buildings that Gropius and Meyer designed for the complex. During this time, Neufert developed a close friendship with Benscheidt Jr. and was a frequent guest at the home of Wilhelm Hanstein, the factory engineer at Fagus. Through these contacts, he became aware of the issues surrounding works organization and standardization. This knowledge was put to practical use in the efficient management of Gropius's practice in 1925–1926 and in the training course at the Staatliche Bauhochschule Weimar directed by Neufert from 1926 to 1930. Moreover, Neufert compiled the experience and knowledge in two volumes entitled *Bauentwurfslehre* (1936) and *Bauordnungslehre* (1943), each seminal works that were enormously influential for decades.

The furniture for Bruno Hans was one of Neufert's earliest works. As it is not mentioned in the archival material on the Bauhaus, we must assume that the designs were drafted in Gropius's office and executed toward the end of 1922 by a local carpenter from drawings that no longer exist. The commission included furniture for each room of the two-bedroom apartment. The solid birch pieces are reminiscent of works by Gropius and Meyer not only in their heavy, cubic volume but also in the finishing details.

Benscheidt Sr. and Jr. were able to interest the later Bauhaus master Hinnerk Scheper (1897–1957), who had just passed his master examination and opened his own studio, in designing the color scheme for the interior. In mid-January 1923, he traveled to Alfeld, where he prepared preliminary designs for all six units and oversaw the interior painting

Apartment building Am Weidenknick. Architect: W. Rudolph, 1922. Factory photo, 1930s.

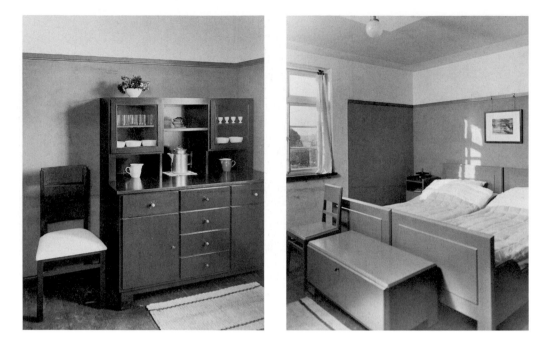

carried out by a local firm, which also stained and varnished the furniture according to Scheper's instructions. He even selected curtains and paintings for Bruno Hans's apartment. The color sketches, preserved in Scheper's estate, show a neutral frieze band above the color treatment of the wall surfaces. This band flowed down to floor level around each window frame. The ceiling mirror was also set off against a light background. Rectangular reflective surfaces surrounded the lighting fixtures in most rooms. The colors included an ochre yellow, several matte green hues, an intense dark blue, and a saturated brown. But photographs of Hans's apartment taken in the fall of 1923 show that the original plan was somewhat modified in the execution.

Scheper's correspondence with his wife tells us how involved Benscheidt father and son were in these tasks: "A huge effort is to be undertaken. . . . Benscheidt wants to show this apartment and the entire house to the public and issue a special invitation to the Industrieverein Alfeld und Umgebung (Industrial Association of Alfeld and Surrounding Area), the Industrieverein Goslar (Industrial Association of Gosslar), the Hanoversche Bauberatungsstelle (Building Counsel of Hanover), Volksbildungsverein (People's Education Association), and union representatives. . . . All this feverish promotion on my, and our, behalf is undertaken at their own initiative. I didn't even have to lift a finger. . . ."[44]

That Benscheidt Sr.'s motives went beyond public relations, that he really wanted to present a new social model, becomes evident in a letter he drafted at age eighty-nine, many years later, in a hospital on June 9, 1947, just a few days before his death. In this letter, he asked that "a temporary home in clay brick construction be built on the property on Weidenknick. It is my wish that this home be realized as quickly as possible and be ready for occupation by fall. If at all possible, the apartment should simultaneously by furnished with pieces in the style previously designed for Mr. Hans in the apartment house on the Weidenknick. I believe that today, more than ever, it is vitally important to set good examples for the general public."[45]

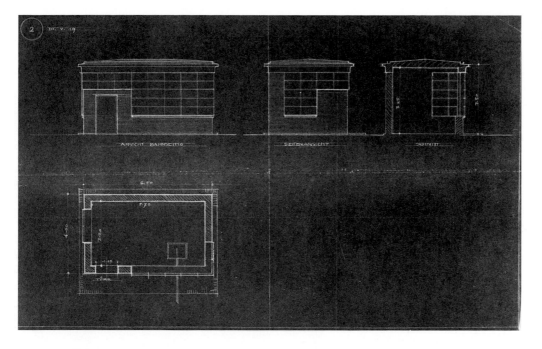

Shunting winch and track scales. Optional design, 1919.

New Buildings, 1923–1925

The building tasks that Gropius and Meyer undertook for Fagus after World War I continued to be on a modest scale. Among them was the building for the shunting winch and the track scales in the east corner of the property. Blueprints in the factory archives indicate that planning began as early as March 1919. The structure had a ground plan no greater than 6.5 m x 4 m, for which the architects handed in three designs options in May 1919. Leather-yellow facing bricks, large windows, and corners without piers identified the structure as part of the Fagus complex. The designs differed mainly in how the glazing was placed. Instead of asymmetric windows, a model that featured a more practical but less creative symmetrical variation was chosen. The small building, completed in late summer 1922, featured a fully glazed wall on the railtrack elevation, wrapping around the two narrow sides. As in the main building, here too the boxed windows appear suspended from the cantilevered lintel like a screen wall in front of the building fabric.

The expansion of the coal and wood-shaving bunker, also located on the track side of the complex, began around 1923–1924. During World War I, a temporary sheltering roof had been propped up on wood posts to gain additional dry storage space—an impromptu response to an immediate need and one that neither Gropius nor Meyer had anything to do with. Several plans from 1920 to 1922 indicate that attempts were underway to modi-

Wood chip bunker and track scales. Photo by Edmund Lill, first half of 1924.

fy this situation. Yet even the
final project, approved by the
building authorities in
December 1923, was only partially executed because of the
currency devaluation.[46]

To avoid slowing produc-
tion, the expansion (as was the
case in 1915–1916 for the boiler and power house) was realized by building around the
existing structure and integrat-
ing it with the overall shape.
The expansion works began in
1924 on the southeast side—
that is, facing the track scales.
In keeping with the function of
a storehouse, wall openings
were restricted to the skylight

area. Instead of a continuous band of glazing wrapping around the corner, which one
might have anticipated after the example set in the boiler house, Gropius and Meyer decided to use individual windows separated by piers. The black, slightly protruding base, the
leather-yellow brick facework, the clean details, and the harmonious proportions integrate
the structure into the complex. At the turn of 1924–1925, a coal bunker reaching down to
basement level was added on the opposite side. It was topped with a reinforced concrete
roof.

The porter's lodge was the last building Gropius and Meyer designed for the Fagus factory. Begun toward the end of 1924, the new building replaced a temporary structure
erected during World War I. The dimension and asymmetrical treatment of the glazing
wrapped around the corner is reminiscent of the optional designs for the track scales. On
this building, however, the flat roof was a slab that reached far beyond the contour of the
building, supported only by a thin wall panel.[47] To ensure optimal entrance and exit control over persons and goods, the south corner of the building was set at an angle. A large
window in the angled wall gave the porter a clear view of the driveway, allowing him to

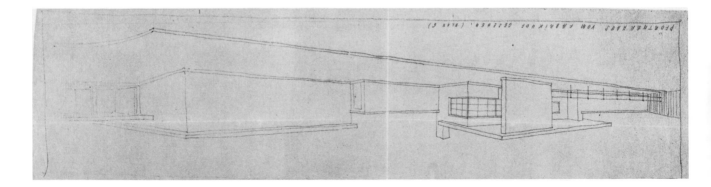

open the electronic gate when necessary. Although the furniture no longer exists, drawings from September and November 1924 document that this building too was furnished with pieces designed in Gropius's office.

With this building, Gropius and Meyer followed models created by De Stijl, especially works by Gerrit Rietveld or Theo van Doesburg and Cornelis van Eesteren. Yet they did not emulate the Dutch manner of dismantling fabrics into open surfaces for the effect of a freestanding sculpture. Rather, Gropius and Meyer merely adopted typical external characteristics, such as the wall and roof slab and the asymmetric placement of the chimney, and combined these elements with the cube with the glazed corner.

Gropius's office delivered drawings for the automatic gate and the enclosure wall at the same time as those for the porter's lodge. A gently curved wall faced in leather-yellow brick bore the lettering "Fagus-Werk Karl Benscheidt," which drew visitors' eyes to the entrance from afar. Photographs from the late 1920s demonstrate the impact of this sober and rational design in the rural landscape. This project was followed by a number of small commissions, mostly related to completing exterior details: lighting for the factory grounds, awnings for the addition to the main building (1925) and the production hall, fencing (1925–1926), and benches and tables for a workers' garden (1926).

Projects for the Clicking-Knife Department, 1923–1925

The clicking-knife department—consisting of tool-and-die shop and forge shop—was the only "old building" that had not been expanded. Years later, Gropius would still state that he had little use for this building because it had turned out too conventional—a personal opinion that makes sense only in hindsight.[48] Despite several attempts, Gropius failed to succeed in reworking this structure, which owed its expression entirely to the prewar era. He tried first in 1913–1914 but was foiled by the outbreak of war, and again between 1923 and 1925, as part of a large-scale project. Had he carried out any of these attempts, the result would have completely changed the image of the Fagus factory.

Documents in the archives tell us how hard Gropius and his team worked to design a new clicking-knife department. The many drafts can be sorted into three planning phases, some with several variations for each phase and for a variety of uses. The earliest draft, a project dated mid-April 1923, still incorporated the original building. The modifications consisted of simplifying the windows and eliminating the sawtooth roof. On the railtrack side, a single-story, fully glazed hall was to be added, whose appearance in the watercolor drawings has some similarity to the power house. The design of the two-story head building, on the other hand, closely echoed the main building, with which it was aligned and to which it was linked via a footbridge from the glazed stairwell on the south corner.

Another draft, created only two days later, shows a recessed mezzanine floor designed as a continuous skylight. In a perspective drawing of the interior by Neufert, we can see that all that would have remained of the original fabric would have been the exterior wall facing the factory. Posts supporting the skylight and girder construction defined the otherwise

Expansion of clicking-knife department, 1st planning phase. Project from April 14 to 17, 1923.

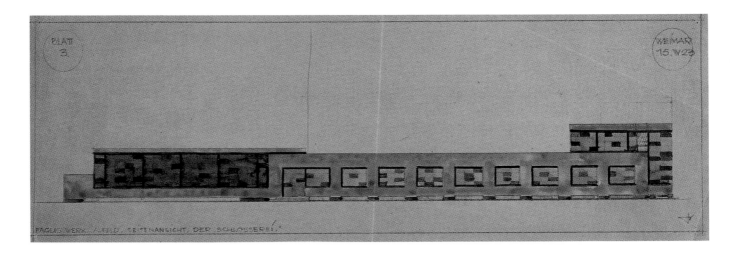

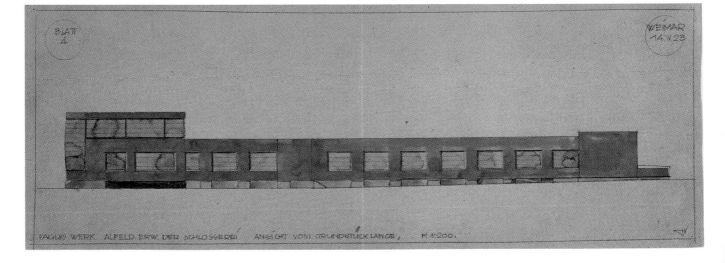

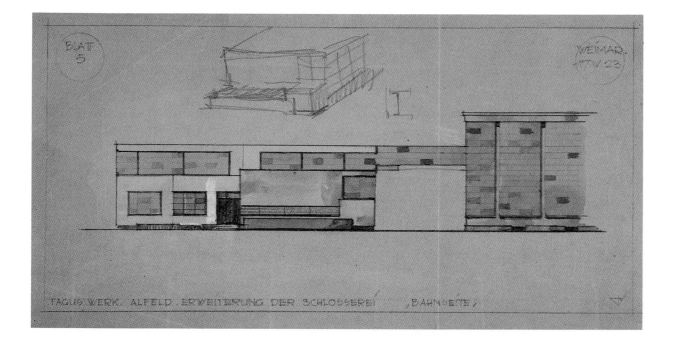

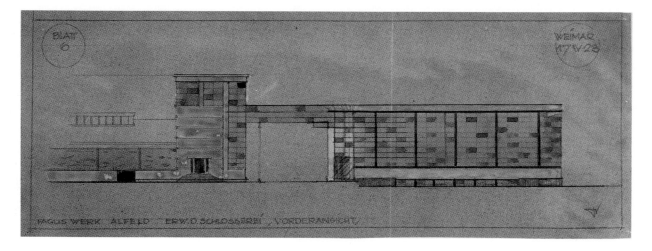

smooth surface that merged with the interior of the additional building on the railtrack side. This was where the tool-and-die shop and the clicking-knife department would have been housed. The head building would have formed an *L* around the old building; it had more harmonious proportions and better-thought-out solutions in the details. The drawings of the imagined railroad elevation, in particular, illustrate the shift from uncertainty to resolution that lies between these drafts, which are only a few days apart.

Both are obviously related to the other buildings of the Fagus factory complex, yet each is distinct. This is especially evident when we compare the main building and the projected head building. Instead of battered piers, the multistory window panels seem merely separated by thin posts. The plan may have envisioned recessing the posts behind the vertical window bands; in the end, however, the glass surface was flush with lintel and parapet. The characteristic plasticity of the window frames, seemingly suspended in front of the wall with beam-shaped end pieces, was not repeated in this structure.

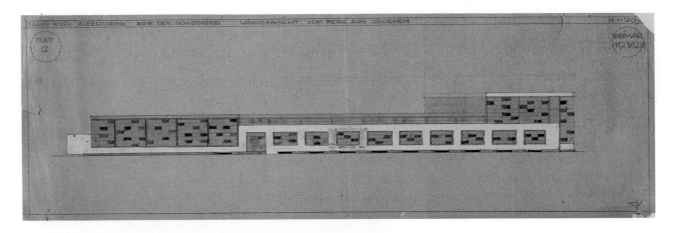

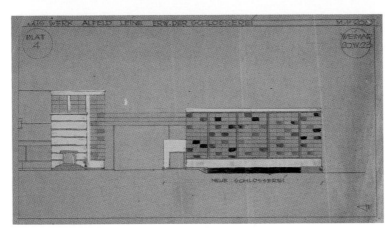

Expansion of punch-knife department, 1st planning phase. Variation drawn April 19–20, 1923. Perspective drawing by E. Neufert.

The drafts for the street elevation (April 1923) were stunningly similar to the later design for the Bauhaus building at Dessau in 1925. The following elements are present in both designs: the dark, recessed, and fully glazed basement level, which gave the building a lightness that was even more apparent than in the main building; the absence of parapets at ceiling level; the flatness of the windows; the absence of dividing brick pillars; the proportions; and, naturally, the use of a bridge structure across an internal street.

While the Fagus factory had been regarded as a precursor to the workshop wing of the Bauhaus building in Dessau since the 1920s, these drafts for the new clicking-knife department mark the decisive halfway point in the development of the curtain wall in the work of Gropius and Meyer; the Fagus factory turns out to have been their arena for experimentation. While the glazing feature was initially reserved for the main building at Fagus—and likewise the office building of the Werkbund factory in Cologne—the architects soon applied it to the production sites and to the outbuildings in the complex. Along the way, they experimented with different structural approaches and design variations. Large glass surfaces, especially when composed of horizontal rectangles, seem to read "factory" in Gropius and Meyer's work. At least the workshop annex in Dessau must be understood as such.

While the subsequent drafts for the new clicking-knife department lack the caution present in the work from April 1923, they are also characterized by a lesser degree of innovation. When an adjacent plot of land came up for sale, the Benscheidts purchased it to gain space for a larger building; this led to renewed efforts to modify the design. All that remains of Neufert's Alfeld concept from early December 1923 are some floor plans. In them one can see that the revised design was based on a completely new building, nearly identical to the main building: recessed piers across three floors between multistory windows and trussless corners. A bridge connected the old and the new building at the old staircase level.

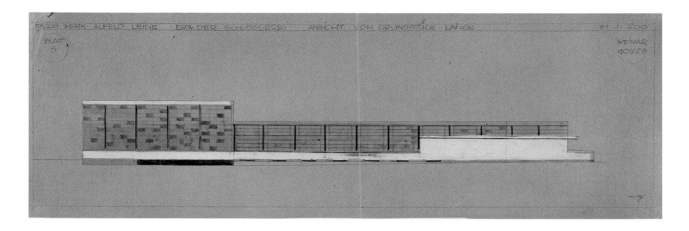

The last and probably ultimate planning phase finally followed in October 1924. The drawings, executed in Weimar, show a three-story-high front building—a true copy of the main building. In an *L*-shape, it surrounds the two-story fabric of the forge shop, which is recessed from the building line and which features—like the power house from 1915–1916—a pillarless glass facade. To differentiate this section as an autonomous production area, a square window format was employed—a return to design features in the existing tool-and-die shop and forge shop from 1911. The bridge was once again envisioned level with the old staircase of the main building.

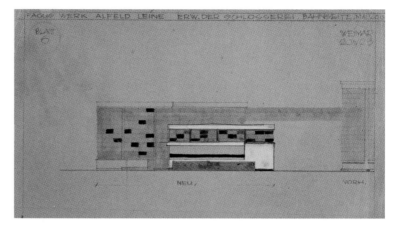

Surprisingly, a drawing of the street elevation contains an optional sketch that would have doubled the size of the clicking-knife department in a mirror-image fashion. The elevation of the railroad side also includes an image of a second warehouse.

Although this mirror-image symmetry must be seen as a return to traditional principles—Gropius and Meyer had already presented the same suggestion for the storehouse of the Kappe company in Alfeld in 1922–1923—in the case of the Fagus factory, it emphasized the identity of the entire complex and confirmed the lasting validity of the older buildings. It is clear from this drawing that the street elevation was interpreted as the main facade.

Drawings continued to be created well into 1925 in Gropius's office, all more or less execution drawings. Then Benscheidt Sr.'s letters to Gropius began to allude to financial strain, which would grow into a full-blown recession in the years that followed. Finally, in 1927, he informed Gropius that all building projects must be put on hold until further notice. A short while later, replying to a letter from a journalist, the sixty-nine-year-old elaborated in uncharacteristic detail on his experiences with Gropius; this letter was a retrospective and critical assessment of what had been achieved at Fagus in the filed of modern architecture: "It comes as no surprise to me that architect Gropius's manner of building is negatively received. Dozens, maybe hundreds of similar letters have been sent to me over the years. This architecture is like all things new; some critics are enthusiastic, others cannot condemn it enough. Furthermore, all new ideas are usually prone to be extreme, and this has also befallen Mr. Gropius. His first drafts were too extreme for my taste as well and, at the time, I rejected many because, on the one hand, I too was not yet ready to embrace the new ideas and, on the other hand, I feared that they would greatly increase building costs, and thus it came that the Fagus factory turned out to be a building that kept its distance from any form of extremism. In this manner, however, it received wide recognition. And yet, were I to build Fagus again today, I would build more extremely than I did then. Today, I recognize that I would have done well to adopt more of Mr. Gropius's ideas."[49]

Indeed, a few years later Benscheidt Sr. endeavored again to build another factory with Gropius in connection with his business affairs in Russia. A draft contract from June 1930 confirms that father and son Benscheidt suggested that a new turnkey production site be built in addition to the extensive technical aid they were providing for the existing state-run last factories. The Fagus factory was presented as the best prototype in all aspects and was introduced in the Soviet Union as the model par excellence. They even went so far as to write into the contract that Walter Gropius be chosen as the architect. These plans were, however, never realized.[50]

In 1936, for the twenty-fifth anniversary of Fagus, Benscheidt Sr. and Gropius resumed contact after several years. In the meantime, Gropius had left Germany and set up a practice in London. From his new professional environment in England—once again, as in 1911, he was asked to modify a factory design by another architect—Gropius summarized his work for Fagus: "I feel now that it was fortuitous that for my first significant building as a young architect I was able to work with you, because, based on your personal experience in life, you had the right understanding for a pioneer approach. I think, further, that you need not have any regrets because the Fagus factory has become known throughout the world also for its visual appearance."[51]

Toward the end of 1936, Benscheidt Sr. asked Gropius anew if he would be interested in working on the expansion of the clicking-knife department. As Gropius still had a work permit and continued to stay in touch with the state authorities in Berlin, this would have been possible, in theory. But Gropius had already decided to accept a position as professor of architecture at Harvard University. Thus he sent Benscheidt a list of names, colleagues whose work he felt comfortable enough to recommend. "Naturally, it is of great importance to me that this expansion be undertaken in a sensitive manner. I believe that Professor Neufert would be a good choice, or Professor Scharoun . . . who would surely approach this task with great tact."[52]

Benscheidt seems to have decided against pursuing the project further and to accept the situation such as it was. Instead, he commissioned Neufert to build a new sawmill. The

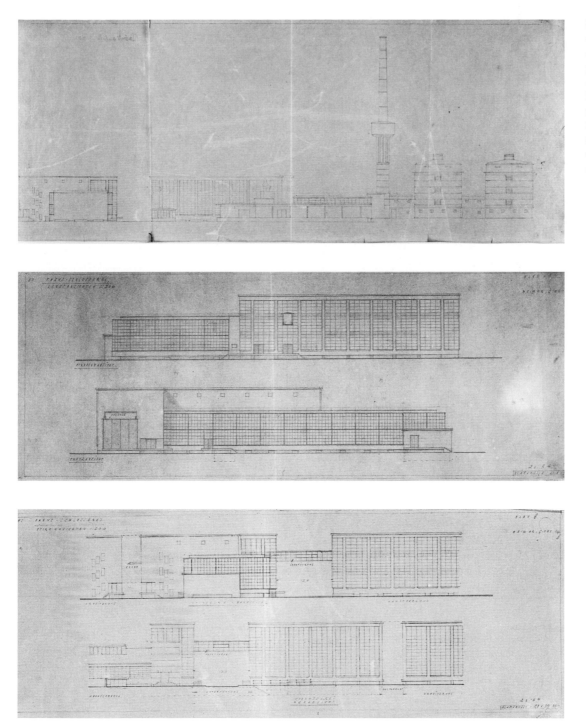

New building for
clicking-knife
department, 3rd
planning phase,
1924–1925.
Railroad
track side.
Longitudinal
sides. Track ele-
vation and street
elevations.

building, its floor space increased by 200 percent in comparison to the original sawmill,
was executed in 1938. Lastly, Neufert also converted one of the garages built in 1912 into a
transformer station. With this conversion, the Fagus factory reached the final state whose
fabric would remain unchanged in the subsequent decades.

Advertising

Architecture as Advertising

The strongest advertising tool for the Fagus factory was its architecture. Even upon founding the company, Benscheidt Sr. planned that he "would spend 20,000 to 25,000 marks annually for advertising alone—in fact, the building itself will be advertising. And it has contributed considerably to making the Fagus factory famous not only within the shoe industry but, I would like to say, across the world."[1]

The architecture of the Fagus factory was an integral part of the company's business philosophy; it embodied modernity, precision, and social progressiveness—qualities that gave insight into the quality of the product. Nearly all expenses for the building could therefore be assigned to the advertising account. For this reason, the sums listed in the annual financial statements under the heading of advertising do not represent the full picture because they were not itemized.

The sophistication of Benscheidt's grasp of advertising strategies is illustrated in the following anecdote. At the beginning of the 1930s, he decided to demolish a signal box near the tracks—it had become nothing more than a storage shed—so that the factory could be

Opposite: Secretary's typewriter table with stationery designed by Johannes Molzahn. Works photo, circa 1927.

The Fagus factory seen from the perspective of a train passenger before and after the switch box demolition. Factory photo, 1930s.

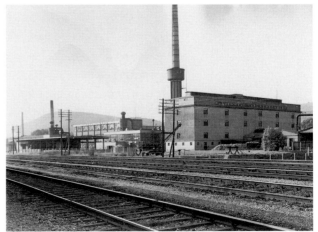

clearly seen from a distance. Benscheidt thought of the 6,000 marks paid to the national railroad service as yet another advertising expense.[2] The view was photographed, at his insistence, in before and after shots, from the perspective of a passenger in an oncoming train. This story is a perfect example of how Benscheidt thought of the railroad elevation as the factory's main facade.

Naturally, the costs for the professional photographs were also allocated to the advertising expense account, as were the many publications about the Fagus factory. On three occasions, detailed accounts of the factory appeared in trade magazines, of which Benscheidt Sr. purchased many copies: 1913 in *Der Industriebau* (1,500 copies), 1925 in *Westermanns Monatshefte* (5,000 copies), and 1930 in the *Schuhfabrikanten-Zeitung* (3,000 copies).[3] This last magazine is identified in Benscheidt's correspondence as having had nearly two years' advance booking. The galleys were sent to Alfeld for approval and released from there for printing. The senior manager described this publication, which he presented as a gift to clients, as "excellent and elegant advertising for the Fagus factory."[4]

The Public Relations Department

Beyond architecture, a company's ambitions and modernity are expressed in the design of its printed matter. They usually create the first impression for a potential client. But in contrast to large companies, Fagus had no in-house advertising department with a staff of graphic designers and copy writers, first and foremost because it was a medium-sized company and also because its market was small and specialized. More than anything else, shoe lasts were an interim product that was never seen by the end consumer. Hence, the advertising needed to be equally specialized. A surprising range of trade magazines covered all aspects of shoe manufacturing.[5]

At Fagus, advertising was handled by the management and Benscheidt Jr. devoted himself to it with keen interest. Over time, he became so skilled and informed that he was a mentor for many of the young designers whom he commissioned. Unfortunately, material on the public relations and advertising work at Fagus is scarce, especially for the prewar era. The archives do, however, contain folders in which the junior manager collected a wide range of ads, primarily from American trade journals. He had obviously observed and studied American methods in advertising, defined by a strong psychological streak, during his year in the United States (1910–1911). Today, the Fagus archives contain few books on advertising. Yet Benscheidt Jr.'s correspondence proves that he often recommended and sent out publications to his ad designers—for example, a copy of Walter Dill Scott's *Psychology of Advertising* (Boston, 1902). Still, as in the case of work organization, it is difficult to determine in hindsight how concrete the American influence on advertising actually was.

From the beginning, Fagus worked together with professional graphic designers. Gropius and Meyer played an important role in establishing contacts with young advertising artists who were still relatively unknown but soon rose to prominence through their work for the Fagus factory. Benscheidt Jr. never employed designers simultaneously; instead, he always worked with one designer at a time, who would handle all the assignments for a given period.

These involved a full range of graphic and corporate design: the printed matter required for daily business interactions—letterhead, invoices, printed forms—advertising brochures, and magazine and newspaper ads. In the mid-1920s, Benscheidt Jr. experimented by giving individual commissions to different artists.

On founding the Fagus GmbH on March 28, 1911, Benscheidt Sr. paid for stacks of printed letterheads and price lists, obviously created without the input of a graphic designer and assembled at the printer, who copied conventional models with standard type from the letter case. Toward the end of 1911, Benscheidt Sr. ran an ad to announce that Fagus was now in operation. The "ad" was, in fact, a response to a call for submissions for "a competition on effective advertisement" in *Schuh und Leder* (Shoe and Leather), a trade publication; the winners were published in the Christmas issue of 1911. Gropius was asked to invite graphic designers from his circle to contribute designs. Benscheidt urged the architect to "please refrain from making any suggestions or stating specific requirements that might influence the artist."[6] Gropius and Meyer recommended Max Hertwig.[7]

Max Hertwig (1881–1975)

A native of Bunzlau, a town in Lower Silesia known for its pottery, Max Hertwig had apprenticed as a printer before attending the School of Arts and Crafts in Düsseldorf from 1902 to 1906. His studies in graphics arts under Fritz Helmuth Ehmcke shaped him into the artist he would become. Next, Hertwig worked as an independent painter and graphic designer in Hanover. From 1908 until 1910, he was employed at Peter Behrens's studio in Neubabelsberg. He taught graphic design, typography, and decorative arts at the Reimann School in Berlin from 1913 to 1933; he also acted as deputy director.

Hertwig belonged to the first generation of German artists trained in graphic design for commercial use. At the School of Arts and Crafts in Düsseldorf, he met Adolf Meyer, whom he befriended when they both worked at Behrens's studio. Gropius and Meyer also

Fagus advertising on the title page of a trade magazine. Design by Max Hertwig, 1913.

Fagus ad. Design by Max
Hertwig, 1912.

supported the graduates of the school;
between 1910 and 1914, they hired a number of designers originating from this
artisitic circle or recommended them to
other studios and companies.[8] With
Hertwig, Fagus found an artist dedicated
to the ideas about graphic design in the
spirit of Ehmcke and Behrens that were
being promoted by the Werkbund. How
vital graphic design was for the sales pro-
motion of a high-quality product should not be underestimated.

By 1912, with the factory up and running, Benscheidt Jr. could focus on advertising.
Hertwig was commissioned to create a coherent visual design for the printed matter. One
of the first projects was the trademark. Hertwig, whose strength was calligraphy, suggested
a handwritten script slanted to the right with long descenders. He developed the script in
several stages on the basis of the initial typeset models. The upper arm of the *F* in the
word *Fagus* was extended to just above the *g*, and the descender of the *g* continued underneath as a kind of underscore line. The result was a dynamic script—not unlike a signature—whose character was individualistic and yet professional.

Benscheidt Jr. reversed the color, printing the script in white on black, which increased its
impact even further, with the negative image virtually leaping out at the reader. The company's logo was placed on the title page of trade publications, which doubled as an advertising
page. Among the badly arranged and designed ads of the competitors, the conspicuous circu-
lar shape of the Fagus ad was generally noticed. In each publication, the script was repeated
on an inside page to reinforce the initial impact. On the last page—sometimes even on the
reverse side of the cover page—the reader, whose interest had already been aroused by the
cover, would then see a larger ad that explained in detail what the word *Fagus* stood for.

Benscheidt Jr. continued to use Hertwig's two ads from 1912 well into the 1920s
because they were so effective, especially in the white-on-black version. Just how successful they were was soon evident when the style was emulated by competitors; thus,
Gustav Berger's shoe-last factory in Erndtebrück, whose name alone, Pegos-Werke, was
a form of plagiarism, ran an ad that was clearly a takeoff of Hertwig's design. Benscheidt
Jr.'s reaction was calm. "For some years, this competitor has given us the pleasure of
copying our ads. . . . *Pegos*, too, is an imi-
tation of *Fagus*; apparently *pegos* is Greek
for beech wood."[9]

In contrast to the Pegos illustration—a
confusing accumulation of buildings drawn
in perspective with excessive detail, eche-
lon, contrast, light, shadow, and depth, all
crowded into a small image—Hertwig
reduced his drawing of the railway elevation to simple outlines, focusing instead on
the dominant architectonic features. Based
on a line drawing from Gropius's office, the

Plagiarized Fagus ad from
Pegos-Werke.

Left: Letterhead. Design by Max Hertwig, circa 1913.

Right: Invoice form for sample lasts. Design by Max Hertwig, 1919.

designer created a compact and flat—that is, graphic—image of the factory complex. Thus, the treatment of the silhouette translated the railroad elevation, and especially the main building at the center, into a memorable image. Hertwig's task was made easier by the pictoral composition of the architecture. The postwar version, with additions and renovations, produced a more complex architecture captured in a drawing that was less succinct and did not have the same powerful impact; the detailed illustration of the glazing in the main building decreased the simplicity of the image.

The Benscheidts tended to focus on the railroad elevation for advertising. As far as we know, this view of the factory was used only once—for the "Musterleisten-Aufstellung" (invoice of prototype lasts) from 1919—in the letterhead. The graphic image of Fagus was different from the then common notion that letterheads with an illustration of one's factory were a particularly effective means of advertising.[10] And yet, although Benscheidt Sr. felt so strongly about the advertising potential of his building, in this area too, as in production and in architecture, his views were clearly distinct from his competitors.

For the letterhead, Hertwig isolated type and color as the sole design elements. In his work for Fagus, he strove to create symmetry through centered justification and evenly distributed weight in each line. Precisely differentiated gradations emphasized highlights in the content: thus the green script "Fagus" was clearly separate from the smaller black lettering, which in turn was divided into bold, regular, or italic attributes and upper and lower case, depending on the importance of the information. No borders or other decorative elements were allowed to interfere with the clear, businesslike statement. On the printed invoice forms with multiple rows and columns, this differentiated typography was too animated, made busier by the ubiquitous quasi-handwritten characters. The Musterleisten-Aufstellung especially seemed to drown in a sea of words and information. In fact, the sheet looked so crowded that it appeared as if it had already been completed.

The Fagus archives contain only a few of Hertwig's advertising brochures designed in 1913–1914. They all had two elements in common: a square format and color combinations of great intensity. With geometric divisions, Hertwig created bordered areas that were rigorously divided into type and ornament and further enhanced by color. Typically, the light centered type stood out against a dark background while the ornamental fields dominated in a saturated lilac or brown combined with black.

After World War I, Hertwig modified the trademark to incorporate the new name, Fagus-Werk, adding "Karl Benscheidt" inside the broad, horizontal extension of the *g* stroke. The resulting materials looked like prewar designs to which the modified logo was added. The most noticeable change was in the choice of color; the letterhead was now printed in a glowing orange instead of green. At the end of the 1919 and beginning of 1920, Hertwig introduced another change to his brochure design: the square gave way to a slender vertical format. Calm, simple shapes replaced the more expressionistic zigzag and strong turquoise took over from the earlier intense but harmonious color combinations.

A few months later, Benscheidt Jr. commissioned Süss, a graphic designer from Munich, to design a brochure for comparison with Hertwig's latest effort. A return to the square format and the familiar border indicate that the junior manager seemed to favor the prewar designs. But Süss's suggestion was not fully convincing either and, in the end, Benscheidt chose to terminate his collaboration with Hertwig and begin afresh with a new designer.

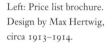

Left: Price list brochure. Design by Max Hertwig, circa 1913–1914.

Right: Shaft models brochure. Design by Max Hertwig, 1919.

Johannes Molzahn (1892–1965)

Johannes Molzahn attended the Grossherzogliche Zeichenschule (Ducal School of Art) in Weimar at a very young age and apprenticed as a photographer from 1906 to 1909. After meeting Oskar Schlemmer, Johannes Itten, and Willi Baumeister in 1912, Molzahn was inspired to try his hand at painting. In 1920, Molzahn left Weimar and settled down in Soest (Westphalia). He began teaching graphic design at the Arts and Crafts School in Magdeburg in 1923 and, in 1928, he accepted a professorship at the State Academy of Fine Art in Wroclaw (Silesia). However, in 1933, Molzahn lost his academic position. He moved first to Berlin and then, in 1938, he emigrated to the United States. Many years later, in 1954, he returned to Germany.

As Molzahn had contacts at the Bauhaus in Weimar, Benscheidt Jr. was probably introduced to him through Gropius and Meyer. The collaboration with Fagus led to an enduring friendship that lasted beyond the intervening war years. Molzahn introduced the junior manager to Ernst Fuhrmann, an author on culture and philosophy and the head of the Auriga publishing house, and may also have introduced him to photographer Albert Renger-Patzsch. Benscheidt Jr. bought some of Molzahn's early paintings and also supported him financially during the difficult years in Berlin.

Letterhead. Design by Johannes Molzahn, 1922.

When Benscheidt Jr. met with Molzahn for initial discussions in March of 1922, the artist's portfolio contained only a few graphic design samples. His work for the Fagus factory established Molzahn as a designer. Karl Benscheidt's correspondence illustrates how the junior manager gradually became Molzahn's mentor.[11] He instructed the artist about the conditions of industrial production, which became the cornerstones of Molzahn's philosophy: "Promotion should be based on the same principles . . . that are true of industry and business: to achieve maximum impact with minimum effort and material."[12]

From the beginning, Molzahn was enthusiastic about an advertising philosophy based on industrial principles. To Benscheidt Jr., he explained, "I am thinking of a style of advertising—more American than America. I want to make advertising into what it should be as it has not yet achieved this level by any means. I am thinking of creating the most rational advertising in the world."[13] This enthusiasm for things American was reinforced by a visit to the Fagus factory in March 1922. Impressed by father and son Benscheidt, Molzahn felt that "they want to lay the foundation for the German shoe industry—that is, to deliver its initiative," a goal in which he was to participate.[14]

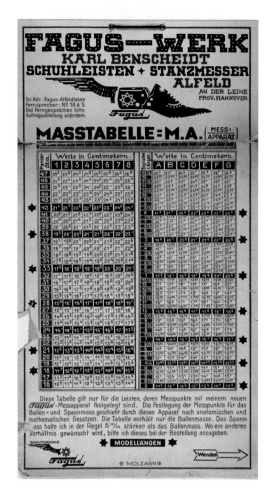

One of Molzahn's first projects was to design a new trademark to add to Hertwig's logo, which was already familiar to clients and industry. Molzahn's idea showed a shoe last decorated with wings and an eight-point star facing right—in the direction of reading. This commodity sign served as a "memorable media component that provides a communication link between industry and consumer"[15] and was used until 1924. The drawing was incorporated into a measurement table (June 1922). This table typified Molzahn's early work: (over)abundant information; varied typography (different font styles, sizes, and attributes); illustrations (including a bird's-eye view of the factory on the reverse side); and multicolor printing.

His first letterhead for Fagus (November 1922) was similarly dense. The centered title "Fagus," with circles and extremely fine lines, posed a difficult challenge to the photoengraver. The ochre yellow set it off against the light blue trademark banderole, which was subtly sketched with delicate strokes. The latter was aligned with the address window of the envelope and served as a background for the address. The lower margin of the sheet was formed by a banderole that combined the Hertwig script and the Molzahn logo, again in ochre yellow, which Molzahn described as the "ultimate industrial color."[16]

This type of comment and, as I have noted, his enthusiasm for technology show that Molzahn's attitude toward industry was more in the vein of romanticizing the machine age than rationally understanding it. This, however, was not in harmony with Benscheidt Jr.'s views; he soon became disenchanted with the designer's work.

In the summer of 1923, Benscheidt informed Molzahn that "in my opinion, your latest designs are no longer sufficiently rational. I feel that we must return to a more serene, dignified, objective form. . . . It is my intention to go to the Bauhaus exhibition week in Weimar. Please let me know whether I will see you there. I hope so, as I would like to invite Mr. Gropius to join in some of our discussions."[17]

Benscheidt Jr. had contacted Gropius as early as May 1922 to discuss Molzahn's design for a billboard. Although neither the draft nor the board survives, we know that it was to be erected in front of the factory. The junior manager told his designer, without further ado, "Gropius is our authority in all questions of taste and especially in all matters that concern our buildings."[18] In January 1923, Gropius and Meyer responded to Benscheidt's request to comment on Molzahn's design for the Fagus business card.

The business card, whose design was revised repeatedly for an entire year, marked the turning point in the commercial graphic design that Molzahn created for Fagus. Finally released for printing in June 1924, it combined the familiar elements of the Hertwig script and the trademark banderole with a rational, blind-embossed grotesque. The rectangular blocks of capitals changed the look of the factory stamp. In combination with the characteristic dots at the beginning of each line, they became a constant element in the subsequent works.

This design appeared for the first time on an accounts receivable statement printed in May 1924. Molzahn varied the font size according to how vital the content was and marked the beginning of each new line with a dot. Even the earliest designs met with Benscheidt Jr.'s approval: "Better than anything we have done thus far."[19] Benscheidt was still wary of overusing the color red. "Red is a dangerous color because it tires the eye. I'm afraid that the bookkeepers who have to fill in accounts all day long will tire and end up making errors."[20] Molzahn adapted his design accordingly by using red only for smaller symbols such as arrows or dots.

Left: Invoice form. Design by Johannes Molzahn, 1924.

Right: Letterhead. Design by Johannes Molzahn, 1924.

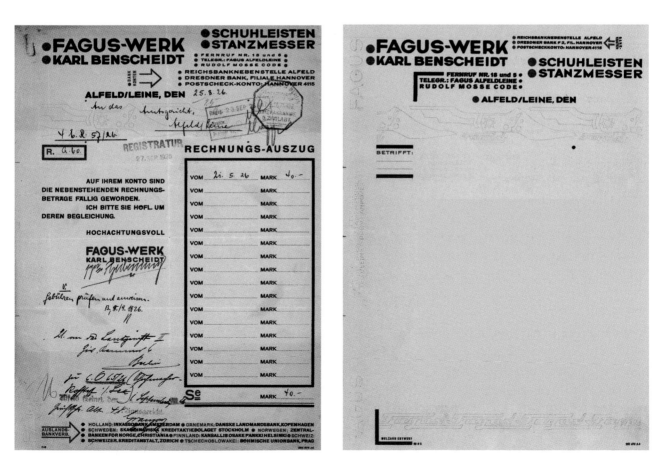

While the layout of the accounts receivable form was confusing and difficult to read, the new letterhead, designed in July 1924, was more convincing. Here the type was transposed and weighted harmoniously, structuring the letter sheet asymmetrically. As in the first letterhead from 1922, Molzahn utilized the trademark banderole—now in delicate gray—as a background for the address label, adding Hertwig's Fagus script in a continuous decorative band along the lower margin. The left margin featured the blind embossing previously printed on the business card. As a new component, Molzahn added right-angle hooks that had a graphic and a practical function: they helped the typist set the margins on the typewriter. Molzahn added his signature inside the angle on the lower margin.

This design was gradually simplified, but its essential characteristics were used well into the 1970s. Benscheidt Jr. soon dropped the blind embossing and the banderole. His correspondence with Molzahn confirms that these reductions were made for aesthetic and financial reasons. The same was true of the red ink, which Benscheidt Jr. used sparingly.

Altogether, Molzahn executed over sixty designs for Fagus by the end of 1928. Among them were ads for foreign markets (Russia, Finland, Austria), which featured the tried-and-true white on black type. By 1925, however, Molzahn's work was mostly restricted to modifying and rereleasing his earlier designs. Around this time, too, Benscheidt Jr. began to commission the Bauhaus directly, most probably as a result of Gropius's influence.

Herbert Bayer (1900–1985)

After the Bauhaus had moved from Weimar to Dessau in 1925, Herbert Bayer was appointed director of its typographic workshop and of the newly founded advertising studio. Before this appointment, in 1919–1920, he had apprenticed in an arts and crafts studio in Linz and then worked in the practice of Darmstadt architect Margold. In 1921–1922, he began studying at the Bauhaus in Weimar. Following his time in Dessau, he spent a decade (1928–1938) as a successful independent graphic designer before moving to the United States.

The earliest documented work by Bayer for Fagus is the business card for Fagus salesman Albert Fesing, a design that must predate August 1925.[21] Because the only remaining card was among Bayer's estate papers, it is reasonable to assume that he designed it. The similarity to Molzahn's postcard from 1923 was surely a result of Benscheidt Jr.'s instructions, extremely pre-

cise as always. Evidently, Bayer was asked to use not only the type but also the type block, which corresponds to the Fagus stamp, the black angle, and dot as well as Hertwig's Fagus script. The red ink used to accentuate individual words wasn't necessarily based on Molzahn's work, but it was an indicator that the management wished to stay with the established corporate design.

On the other hand, the small format of the card was simply burdened with too much information and a confusing array of fonts; all in all, the design failed to convince. From a client perspective, the Fagus logo was too inconspicuous. Benscheidt Jr. must have criticized the design, because many of the cards were "recycled" and used in Albers's elementary course at the Bauhaus for student exercises. The cards had not been printed at the Bauhaus print shop,[22] which rules out the possibility that the students were simply using overstock. Instead, this was probably an earlier edition of cards put to creative use.

Using the same slightly modified sans-serif font, Bayer subsequently designed ads for the Fagus factory with exclusively uppercase type. In the horizontal rectangular format, the bold upper line FAGUS was now dominant, in black-on-white or vice versa; below it, several other lines were printed in a smaller font size, in some instances again divided by angles or dots. Four print matrixes for combination are preserved in the Fagus archives. The earliest known publication of one of these ads was on the title page of *Die Schuh-Post*

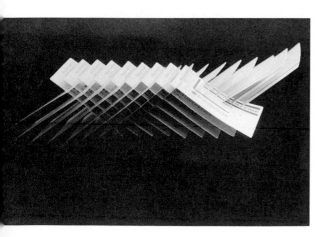

(The Shoe Post), a trade magazine, on October 10, 1925. By inference, we can date the original design accordingly.[23] Bayer was, in fact, completing a project that Molzahn had started at the beginning of 1925.[24]

After 1925, Bayer designed several four-page folding brochures in DIN A 5 format based on the previous ads; their common characteristic was a vertical red stroke along the right edge of the front page. FAGUS was used as a bold label and the name of the relevant product was below in

Fesing business card. Design by Herbert Bayer (?), 1925.

Student exercise with samples of Fesing business card at the Bauhaus in Dessau, elementary course taught by Josef Albers.

smaller type. As I have already mentioned with regard to the business card for Albert Fesing, Bayer utilized Molzahn's familiar designs for the two inside pages and the rear page, although he managed to package them with "increased visual intensity"[25] by creating a dramatic effect commensurate with the text through open spaces, colors, and symbols: angle, arrow, dot, question mark, and bar.

Bayer's estate papers also included a proof for the "Schaftmodelle" (shaft models) brochure designed in 1925.[26] Because the print credit reads "bauhausdruck.bayer" (printed by Bauhaus) in the lowercase type introduced after mid-September 1925, the design must have been created in the fall of 1925.[27]

Fagus ad on title page of trade magazine. Design by Herbert Bayer, 1925.

Many copies of this brochure are preserved in the Fagus archives from a rerun printed at the local print shop, called Stegen, in Alfeld. The cards from the rerun are identical to the originals with the exception of the print credit.

The same applies to the much simpler "Stanzmesser" (clicking-knife) brochure. Two examples of this design appear in Bayer's estate, one of them an improved version (with new type and stand).[28] This may be a work created in Bayer's advertising class at the Bauhaus. Some time later, this brochure was newly typeset and printed once again at Stegen in Alfeld, naturally without the "BAUHAUSDRUCK" credit. The archives contain yet another version, with a fully revised text on pages two to four; this last version was probably created soon after the previous two.

Finally, again from Bayer's estate, there is a copy of a single page sheet entitled "Stützmesse" (safety knife), marked "BAYER BAUHAUS" and dated (by hand) 1926.[29] Here Bayer incorporated a photograph, which he framed horizontally and vertically in type instead of the right-angle hooks that were used before. This card also exists in a second, modified version with new typesetting and the heading "Sicherheitsmesser." For the second card, the original image was exchanged for a photo from Renger-Patzsch's 1928 Fagus series that shows the object from a higher perspective.[30] Again, the reprint was carried out by the print shop Stegen in Alfeld.

Additional archival material includes brochures entitled "Hirnholz-Stanzklötze und Zuschneidebretter" and "Miller Aufblock-Maschinen" cutting blocks and boards; Miller "treeing" machines); while these were not actually designed by Bayer, they were modeled on his work, probably in the years leading up to 1930. Although the brochures and the single sheet are unquestionably part of a series, one wonders at the difference in their execution. This is especially true for the Fagus logo on the title page; Bayer's three designs and the Bauhaus designs all used different fonts. The lack of consistency may have caused Benscheidt Jr.'s dissatisfaction and his decision to end the collaboration, probably as early

as 1926.[31] The degree of his influence on the design of these brochures is palpable in the correspondence even today. The junior manager most certainly chose both the copy and the concept; the archives revealed numerous advertising slogans and ad copy text in Benscheidt Jr.' handwriting, all dated after the mid-1920s.[32]

The concept of folding brochures began with Fagus and Molzahn. In December 1924, the works engineer suggested creating a catalog with individual folders for eight product groups, each bearing a strip of color along the right edge of the sheet. The colors were based on Oswald's color circle. The DIN A 5 format and the perforations along the left edge were also fixed design elements.[33] Molzahn completed a design for the "Stützmesser" prospectus in early 1925. In the absence of a preserved copy or any other documentation, it is impossible to determine whether or not this design was ever printed.

The overall impression is that the collaborative efforts of Benscheidt Jr. and Molzahn were presented to the Bauhaus as the graphic corporate image par excellence. The junior manager was often the more astute of the team; one example of this is his decision to use the DIN paper format as early as February 1924. On the other hand, Gropius and Meyer acted as consultants after 1922 and many of their suggestions had a lasting influence on the Fagus graphics. Laszlo Moholy-Nagy, whom Benscheidt Jr. also knew—at least according

Brochures. Designs by Herbert Bayer and others, 1926.

to his address book—was probably another source of inspiration. In the end, however, it is impossible to distinguish to what degree each of the many participants actually did contribute. This may be another reason for the inconsistency in the execution.

Theo van Doesburg (1883–1931)

In January 1925, Karl Benscheidt Jr. attended a lecture by Dutch artist Theo van Doesburg in Hanover. When the artist spoke of Fagus as an "example of good building,"[34] the junior manager spontaneously invited him to visit the factory. Van Doesburg arrived in Alfeld on January 28, 1925, accompanied by Kurt Schwitters. Both artists were treated to a guided tour and then invited to dinner. During the meal, van Doesburg was commissioned to design a Fagus ad for French and Belgian trade publications.

Ad for French market. Design by Theo van Doesburg, 1925.

Van Doesburg's estate contains several proofs for the ad.[35] Using two photographs of a Fagus last fastened to a heel-standardizing bench, van Doesburg simply inserted white arrows to emphasize the foot-friendly characteristics of the Fagus product. The unusual placement of the words, Fagus-Werk, the vertical Molzahn type block (Fagus stamp), and the compactness of the typeset text all animate the asymmetric composition. In Germany, the ad was probably published only in *Offset*, a magazine for graphic designers. The *Offset* ad did not include the copy text on the bottom left. The copy praised the perfection of the Fagus shoe last as a result of science, art, and practical experience. The arguments and the manner of expression indicate that this was probably one of Karl Benscheidt Jr.'s texts in translation. At the beginning of 1929, however, Benscheidt had to tell van Doesburg that Fagus was unable to introduce its products on the French market and, soon after, he stopped trying to place more of the ads.[36]

Karl Benscheidt Jr. as Graphic Designer

With the onset of the recession and the depression after 1926, the junior manager began to handle print design and production himself. He utilized the old Hertwig designs (ads from 1912 and 1919) and Molzahn graphics (letterhead and all office papers), sometimes producing straightforward reruns of the original and sometimes updated or modified versions.

Sales folders and folding brochures based on Bayer's work fall into the latter category. Benscheidt preferred Molzahn's graphics consisting of text block (Fagus stamp), hook, arrow, and dot, but also liked to use Hertwig's scripted logo.

To Benscheidt, these were "universal clichés," as he called them in his correspondence with Molzahn as early as 1922, which he was free to combine and use as needed, adding or rewriting the copy when necessary. In the years that followed, Benscheidt Jr. concentrated on typesetting. This approach more or less eliminated the need for a graphic designer. At the same time, the junior manager delegated the technical tasks, such as ad production and correspondence, to the works engineer, whose rationalization efforts extended to the public relations department.

A series of ads appeared after 1928 whose copy was written in a persuasive style. The advertising files in the archives contain many copies of this series. In some instances, the junior manager submitted his ad campaigns to professional copy writers, who criticized his excessively rational or objective logic. By the beginning of the 1930s, Benscheidt Jr. integrated photographs into his designs. In doing so, he always took care to place the ads in an exposed position, preferably on the title page and in large format. One must emphasize that the Fagus advertising strategy was only partially driven by graphic design; effective placement was as, if not more, important.

Plagiarized letterhead after a Fagus design by Johannes Molzahn.

Anyone looking at those trade magazines today will notice the restraint (no promises of miracle cures) and the contemporary look of the Fagus ads. Benscheidt Jr. was a pioneer of modern advertising in the shoe industry. If any more proof were required, one need only look at how many elements from Fagus ads were emulated and even plagiarized. Hertwig's script and ad were not the only instances; soon Molzahn's letterhead was also copied. A Polish salesman who worked closely with the Fagus factory was one culprit, the other being a shoe manufacturer in Wesphalia. But the aforementioned Pegos-Werke whose plagiarism was, if this were possible, even more obvious: an undisguised copy of the brand logo. Fagus was a groundbreaking enterprise, in advertising just as much as it had been in any other respect.

Fagus and Photography

Photography for Advertising and Documentation

From the beginning, photography fulfilled two roles at Fagus: advertising and documentation. The quantity and quality of the photographs in the factory archives is tangible proof, even now, of how interested Benscheidt Sr. and Jr. were in photography. While professionals were put in charge of capturing the factory's architecture on film, an in-house but otherwise unknown photographer handled all internal requirements after 1920. One of his tasks was to take product shots and to photograph day-to-day operations. The advent of the precision lathe and the growing product range in the area of mechanical engineering expanded the photographer's range after the late 1920s; the Fagus flyers always included photographs of the relevant product or machine. The quality of these shots was frequently as good as those done by professionals. As we have seen in the context of advertising copy, here too the amateur observed and learned from the professional.

At the center of attention stood Albert Renger-Patzsch, supported by Benscheidt Jr. through the purchase of individual prints and referrals,[1] one of which may have led to the work for Dr. Weinert that began in 1926. Although calling the junior manager a collector would be an exaggeration, the 1928 Fagus series by Renger-Patzsch seems to have been commissioned with more than just business interests in mind. Obviously, the images were also valued for their artistic character. The many prints preserved in Dr. Weinert's estate are further proof of how appreciated Renger-Patzsch's creative ability was, as is the fact that the photographer was asked to create a second series in the fall of 1952.

The factory photo archives contain copies of photographs for publicity as well as for in-house use, but also simple snapshots of friends and acquaintances of the Benscheidts. Among them are two small photographs that El Lissitzky took when he visited Alfeld in September 1926. Although these are better categorized as amateur snapshots of the factory gate and the power house, the junior manager not only filed them, he even asked the in-house photographer to work with the same motif. While El Lissitzky used a steep upward angle to capture the pattern of the coffered ceiling, the in-house photographer chose to do a closeup of the machine.

Opposite: Fagus ironing tools. Photo by Albert Renger-Patzsch, April 1928. Fagus series no. 44.

Machine house. Top: Photo by El Lissitzky, 1926. Bottom: Factory photo, late 1920s.

The oldest images in the Fagus archives show that Benscheidt Sr. appreciated the documentary value of photography even in his early days as managing director at the Behrens shoe-last factory; a set of prints, some mounted on cardboard, of the new plant built in 1897 and subsequent additions document his activities as manager and overseer of the factory construction. These prints show panoramic views of the complex as well as images of the individual buildings, usually taken from a greater distance. The commissioned photographers tended to work from a 45-degree angle so as to capture the building in an oblique view. Front elevations and detail closeups were less interesting; what did matter, however, was documenting the whole: the order and size of the factory complex in the image as a projection of the economic strength and solidity of the enterprise.

At Behrens, only the completed building was photographed, but at Fagus, the construction was photographed as well. Although customary to document how a building was realized from foundation to completion, this was a more common approach in the case of public buildings, structures that were particularly interesting from a structural or architectural point of view, and large-scale industrial plants. For Benscheidt Sr., the photographs were a means of keeping his American partners informed about the progress in the construction; moreover, they were an outward expression of his conviction that he was creating an extraordinary building.

Images of the finished factory were first published in 1913 in *Der Industriebau*, a magazine for architects, engineers, and factory owners.[2] It is interesting to note that the first in-depth article on the Fagus factory was not published in a trade magazine for the shoe industry.[3] Benscheidt was already familiar with *Der Industriebau* prior to meeting Gropius, but the initiative for the feature seems to have come from the architect. Gropius had already submitted two articles, essays on industrial architecture, for different issues in 1912.[4] The article on Fagus must have seemed like a demonstration of how to translate his theories into practice. Benscheidt's interests too were satisfied; the detailed description and illustration of the production process was unusual for this type of magazine, and images of the Fagus factory itself were never again reproduced in such detail.[5]

Shoe Last Factory. C. Behrens. Photo by E.P. Freche.

It seems that Gropius even selected the photographer for this publication. His activities at the Deutscher Werkbund and the Deutsches Museum für Kunst in Handel und Gewerbe had given him an early awareness of how important good photography was in the presentation of architecture. At around this time, Gropius began to build a carefully sorted image archive of his own work. He continued to build on it throughout his long career and successfully influenced how others wrote about him and his buildings by supplying them with selected prints from his own archives. Benscheidt also understood the need for good photography in advertising. He was pleased at the interest generated through the young and relatively unknown architect. Edmund Lill, a photographer from Hanover, was hired to document the Fagus factory until the mid-1920s. The same photographer had already worked for Gropius and Meyer once before; in 1911 he had photographed their interior design of the Herzfeld flat in Hanover.[6]

Edmund Lill (1874–1958)

As Edmund Lill described in his memoirs,[7] even as a child he had enjoyed the smell of colophonium that influenced his childhood decision to become a professional photographer. His uncle and three of his siblings were already established in the profession. Lill's training followed the usual path of apprenticeship in several photo studios. At sixteen, he completed his training under Katarina Cuillier, who specialized in child portraiture in Frankfurt/Main, and then worked as a printer in various German cities. Gradually he advanced to head printmaker, left the laboratory, moved into studio work, and finally rose to become managing director of his brother Hubert Lill's photography business in Stuttgart (1863–1934).[8]

Taking over the Tiedemann studio in Hanover, Edmund Lill went independent in 1908. In addition to portrait photography he began to focus on still and architectural photography. In 1927, having lost his entire fortune in the wake of the currency devaluation, Lill decided to branch out into photography supplies and opened a store in the new Bahlsen building. The fact that the studio was located in just such a building and that Friedrich Vordemberge-Gildewart designed an advertising campaign for Lill give us an idea of how open he was toward the modern movement in Hanover. Although Lill described himself as an "expert in architecture and industrial photography,"[9] he never limited his work to this sector.

From 1912 to 1925, Edmund Lill produced some one hundred photographs of the Fagus factory. Only a small number are stamped, but most are identifiable by the five-digit plate number on the reverse side. In combination with the construction dates, each photograph can be dated to a specific year.[10] Vintage prints have been preserved in the Fagus archives and in Walter Gropius's and Adolf Meyer's estates.[11]

The Benscheidts commissioned Lill to document the completion of each new building. His first work for Fagus was probably the 1912 photo series for publication in *Der*

East facade seen from railtrack. Photo by Edmund Lill, 1912.

Industriebau.[12] In contrast to his later work, this was a comprehensive documentation of the factory as a whole, the building as well as the individual production phases. All subsequent Lill photographs were exterior shots or shots of the executive offices designed by Gropius.

Because the completion of the expansion begun in 1913–1914 was delayed through World War I, Lill's next commission did not arrive until May 1922. This time he focused on the street elevation. The crisp, clear images show that the addition to the main building was still unfurnished at this point; a wood scaffold can be seen in the staircase, whose walls are yet to be finished, and the door opening into the vestibule is covered by a plain plywood door labeled "Do not enter."

After the small building for track scales was completed, photographs were taken in 1922 of the factory elevation on the railroad side. Special attention was paid to the boiler and power house. Neither this nor the other folders were ordered into a specific sequence. These weren't series per se to document the factory in step-by-step closeups; rather, the changes in perspective singled out the photographs as autonomous portraits—as common

Boiler house and power house. Photo by Edmund Lill, November 1922.

Full view, from the south. Photo by Edmund Lill, May 1922.

in architectural photography as was Adolf Meyer's trip to Alfeld to instruct Lill on the angle and position he was to use for each shot.[13]

During the first half of 1923, pictures were taken of the newly completed interior of the main building. The portfolio included shots of the vestibule on the ground floor, the stairwell, the hallway, and the offices in the addition. The kitchen in Benscheidt Jr.'s home, which Gropius and Meyer renovated gradually over the course of several years, was also photographed.

By September 1923, the interior of the corporate housing at Am Weidenknick, which had been furnished by the Bauhaus, was photographed, as were atmospheric views of Alfeld and surroundings. The photographs were executed under the direction of Ernst Neufert, who was also in charge of designing the furniture in the company apartment.

Main staircase. Photo by Edmund Lill, first half of 1923.

Full view from railtrack side. Photo by Edmund Lill, first half of 1924.

During the first six months of 1924 additional shots of Alfeld were taken—for example, of the houses erected by the builder's cooperative—while the factory itself was photographed only intermittently. One print is a corner shot of the main building with an electric trolley passing in the foreground; this is probably the most frequently reproduced image of Fagus and fifty-seven prints survive in the Fagus archives alone. A number of additional prints show a variation on this theme, with other trucks in front of the building.

Photogravure plates and sepia prints underscore how important these photographs were to the business. Some of them bear notations on the back, such as "This photograph does not need to be returned," meaning that the image should be reproduced and distributed. No other photograph by Lill so emphasized the modernity of the company, which is why Benscheidt Jr. used it repeatedly in ads and on postcards. The full impact of the image is made even clearer when one looks at an ad by the Behrens company from the same period (still done with a drawing), which illustrated how the goods were transported within the factory grounds by horse and wagon.

After the courtyard was paved and the porter's lodge completed, Lill took the last photographs of the street elevation in November 1925. Now that the factory complex had reached a preliminary stage of completion, his task for Fagus was at an end.

In all his pictures, Edmund Lill tried to communicate the architectural coherence of the Fagus complex. The wide angle, at times also the elevated viewpoint, gave him an unfettered perspective of the whole complex. To begin with, he photographed the complex in full and in half frames. After the fall of 1922, he began to photograph individual buildings. Lill nearly always positioned himself at a 45-degree angle to the building; even when shooting interiors, he would choose an oblique view to capture as much as possible in one image. This approach continued in the tradition of nineteenth-century architecture photography and was no different from what had been done for the Behrens factory. The same can be said of the decision to make sepia and Koppmann prints of especially successful shots, whose brownish patina was meant to invest the image with solidity and artistic flair. Edmund Lill was a versatile technician and an excellent documentary architecture photographer. Today, his photographs are an invaluable source for the upkeep of the factory because of their depth, focus, and readable details.

However, it would be unfair to describe Edmund Lill solely as a good craftsman without innovative spark. The Fagus portfolio after 1922—for example, the frontal views of interiors—explored new ways of seeing. A true change in Lill's self-perception as a photographer was noticeable after 1925, when he moved away from the horizontal full or half-frame and began to render details in stunning vertical compositions.

An interior view of the power house and an oblique view of the main building with the electric trolley in the foreground stand out among the Fagus photographs, less because of their perspective than their interpretative content. Workers were no longer asked to pose in front of the building to demonstrate scale, as had still been the case in the photographs taken in 1912. Instead, they continued with their task in a natural manner, even though it was choreographed for the shot. As members of a modern, technological, and professional world, they were active subjects, masters of machinery. This status is due to the clean energy provided by electricity, symbolized in the generator and the electric trolley; in the Fagus factory, heavy physical labor by the sweat of the brow was a thing of the past. The future in factory work had arrived. The new work was a matter of operating and monitoring machinery, and an architecture suffused with light was the perfect setting for a socially reformed corporate culture based on modernity and efficiency. The pathos in the photograph of a machine operator seen from behind and silhouetted against the steep vertical glass wall was tangible; it stood as a metaphor for faith in humane progress. The space and light of the architecture evoked the advent of a liberated and better world: the world of modern technology.

These images capture our imagination even today.[14] This is not only because they have been frequently reproduced and are therefore lodged in our memory but also because of the clear message they convey. By contrast, Renger-Patzsch's photographs were more demanding of the viewer and of a more intellectual nature.

Albert Renger-Patzsch (1897–1966)

Albert Renger-Patzsch's interest in photography was awakened by his father, an amateur photographer who taught him the practical side of his future profession. After World War I, Renger-Patzsch studied chemistry, but broke off before graduating. Instead, he worked as the director of the Folkwang image archives in Hagen from 1922 to 1924. There he worked closely with the author and director of Auriga Verlag, Ernst Fuhrmann, who intro-

duced him to Johannes Molzahn. Together they published several books. After 1925, Renger-Patzsch worked as a freelance photographer, residing first in Bad Harzburg until November 1929, then in Essen, where he taught photography at the Folkwang school in 1933–1934. His appointment as lecturer was cut short, however, by the political circumstances. After the publication of *Die Welt ist schön* (The World is Beautiful) in late 1928, Renger-Patzsch was regarded as the leading photographer of the Neue Sachlichkeit (New Objectivity) not least because of his Fagus photographs, which were included in the book. Karl Benscheidt Jr. was introduced to the photographer by Molzahn in 1926 and the two remained friends well into the 1950s.

Fagus Series, 1928

No letters or other documents survive that would help us reconstruct why Albert Renger-Patzsch was commissioned to create a photo series of Fagus. This was probably an executive decision to obtain first-rate images for use in advertising. Regardless of its genesis, the series counts among the best work ever done in modern photography.

Contrary to the commonly held opinion that the Fagus photographs date from 1926–1927, I believe that they were taken in April 1928.[15] This may come as a surprise. After all, we know that the company was in the red after 1926, that its archives were already full of excellent photographs by Lill, and that Fagus employed an in-house photographer. Obviously, the plan was to use Renger-Patzsch's unusual images to draw

Porter's lodge. Photo by Albert Renger-Patzsch, April 1928. Fagus series no. 4.

attention to the company outside of Germany; advertising campaigns in the form of illustrated serial ads were to help capture new markets.[16]

Until now, only a few of the photographs, albeit the most famous, have been known to the wider public, and these were taken out of context. The Fagus series consists of at least fifty-four photos that show products and parts, steps in the last-making process, factory architecture, and even portraits of the factory owners. The prints are numbered on the back, making it easy to establish the sequence. Some photographs from Gropius's and Meyer's

View down into stairwell. Photo by Albert Renger-Patzsch, April 1928. Fagus series no. 10.

estates can be added to the portfolio in the Fagus archives, bringing the total number of motifs known at this time to forty-two.[17] In addition, of two unnumbered photographs, one—a closeup of a stack of rough lasts—belongs unquestionably to the series taken in 1928. The other photograph shows a beech forest and was published on the occasion of the twenty-fifth anniversary publication for the Fagus factory.[18] Yet another image, published in 1929 but not filed in the Fagus archives, depicts workers rearranging beech logs in the factory yard.[19] The format of most of the prints is a larger one preferred by Renger-Patzsch (approximately 23 cm x 17 cm); a number of smaller prints can be counted as contact prints (11 cm x 8 cm).

The architecture was the dominant feature, to begin with. The series started out with a photograph of the enclosure wall (see page 3). The factory sign reading "Fagus-Werk Karl Benscheidt" served as the title for the series; it indicated the topic and the factory owner. The inscription "Schuhleisten und Stanzmesserfabrik" (shoe-last and clicking-knife factory) attached to the roof of the warehouse prepared the viewer for the product range presented in the shots that followed. The portraits of Benscheidt Sr. and Jr. set the final accent, providing a tie-in with the bottom line in the title image; the series comes full circle, having illustrated every aspect of the wording in the first photograph.

Renger-Patzsch set out to follow a logical course through the factory grounds; after the entrance, he photographed the porter's lodge (numbers 3 and 4), then the main building—first in the context of the street elevation, then a closeup of the corner without piers and details—and, finally, an overall view of the entire complex (numbers 7 to 9). Next, Renger-Patzsch's lens guided his viewers through the main entrance. The first interior shot was a vertical view down the length of the multistory glass skin, taken from a landing (number 10). We can just glimpse of the tip of the photographer's shoe in the bottom left of the image, a subtle but necessary orientation aid.

On the third floor, Renger-Patzsch captured a group of apprentices in a frame that showed them working on drawings in the brightly lit vestibule with natural light flowing in through the glazing on three sides (number 12). This photograph was an exception within the series in that people were shown in connection with the factory. We can assume that Benscheidt Jr., who was very involved in the training and workers' education offered at the factory, may have been the driving force behind this shot, which featured both modern teaching methods and the multiple uses of the architecture. The next photograph illustrated—from an apprentice's perspective, one might say—the view of the west corner without piers, framed and divided by the gridwork in the windows (number 13).

Continuing on his tour, Renger-Patzsch entered the office area in the main building, photographing the tract that overlooked the railroad (number 14). Although the corridor had natural light penetrating from two sides, it appeared dark and endlessly long. Next, the photographer stepped out of the main building to shoot the northeast facade (number 15). Turning around, he captured the southeast facade in an almost parallel view. This image (number 16; see page 121) would become the most effective view of the Fagus factory, influencing how the architecture was received and interpreted.

Continuing along the northeast side, Renger-Patzsch passed by the boiler house and the power house reached the warehouse (number 18). This composition was especially successful: a shot from inside the shaded wood-chip bunker onto the boiler house with the main building rising behind it. The cantilevered concrete roof obliterated and blacked out the narrow strip of sky along the top edge of the image (number 17). This was the last of the architectural shots in the series.

The clock on the main building, proves that the display sequence of the first nine shots did not reflect the sequence in which Renger-Patzsch took them. Instead, the num-

Boiler house and main building. Photo by Albert Renger-Patzsch, April 1928. Fagus series no. 17.

bering was an attempt to reconstruct the guided tour a visitor would take through the factory. All the more astonishing, then, that no such sequence was applied to the subsequent photographs. Without any recognizable pattern or logic, from image number 19, followed by one grouping after another. Some were undoubtedly images that were meant to stand on their own, while others were obviously intended for advertising. Some fit into both categories.

Among the latter were product shots. Feature images of the ironing tool form B (numbers 43 and 44), the double socket for electrical ironing equipment (number 45), the Miller twin-treeing machine for boot production (number 36), as well as the Fagus clicking knife (number 41) could have been intended for the advertising campaign with alternating ads mentioned in the previous chapter. They were accompanied by ad copy, and while each could stand on its own, together they formed a catalog of Fagus products. With the help of drafts of ads in Benscheidt Jr.'s advertising folder and what we know of the product range at the factory, we can reconstruct which images are missing in the series: ironing tool form E, upper

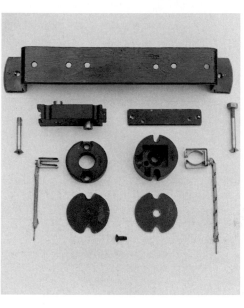

Fagus double socket and parts. Photos by Albert Renger-Patzsch, April 1928. Fagus series no. 45 and no. 48.

leather cutting knife, shaft models, soles. Some of the images were obviously intended for a variety of purposes—for example, for a catalog of spare parts for ironing tools (numbers 44 and 47) and the matching double sockets (numbers 45 and 48). The clear arrangement of the individual parts in the shot followed standard procedure in catalog photography at the time.[20]

The Fagus files contain an early concept sketch for an advertising campaign (1919) that aimed at presenting a kind of visual storyboard of how shoe lasts were manufactured.[21] This, too, could easily be reconstructed using the photographs by Renger-Patzsch (see pages 18 and 19): the beech forest (unnumbered), the cut lumber in the Fagus yard (number 27), restacking the lumber prior to processing (number 28), cutting the wood into foot-size wedges (number 29), storing the rough lasts (number 22 and unnumbered), shaping the last on the lathe (number 31), personal quality control carried out by the junior manager (numbers 38 and 39), and finally, shipping (number 23).

We can only speculate what the photographs were actually used for, because only one product shot from the Fagus series is documented as having been used for advertising: a shot of a clicking knife in the summer re-edition of the "Stanzmesser" brochure originally designed by Herbert Bayer in 1926. In the new version, the older cliché was replaced with

G 356

photograph number 41. It is possible that the depression put an end to plans for other ad campaigns.

The hesitation in using the Fagus photographs may, however, also have been a matter of their suitability for advertising. A large portfolio of photographs was dispatched, for example, at the beginning of January 1930 for inclusion in the report on the Fagus factory to be published in the trade magazine *Schuhfabrikanten-Zeitung*, yet few of these shots were taken by Renger-Patzsch.[22] Benscheidt Sr. made a point of stressing with the editorial department that the photograph he had first sent publication—"image Fagus 34," a shot of a heel-standardizing machine—"was unsuitable for the purpose."[23] It was exchanged for a picture taken by the in-house photographer that featured the company name more prominently. The artfully composed image number 32, hardly appropriate for selling the measuring-point marking machine pictured in it, bears even less visual information. In this case, the in-house photographer's work was the obvious choice; the shot was technically expert even though its composition was very conventional. The second photograph was more effective because there was no attempt at staging the object. This was a purely documentary photograph without artistic ambitions.

Renger-Patzsch's architectural photographs elicited similar reactions. Obviously, father and son Benscheidt preferred the clarity of Lill's work. Nevertheless, Renger-Patzsch's series was widely distributed through Gropius and his circle. Most importantly, however, these images promoted a new way of looking at and of interpreting the architecture of the Fagus factory.

New Objectivity in Photography and Architectural Interpretation

As Renger-Patzsch would later observe, in photographing architecture he always began with a close study of the relevant building. He was categorically opposed, however, to consultation between photographer and architect and to set prerequisites with regard to perspective and position. This resistance to outside influences was his way of preserving a measure of unaffectedness that would protect him from becoming an advertising agent on behalf of the architect.[24] And yet the Fagus series did just that.

Each frame was carefully chosen, each picture composed with precision; Renger-Patzsch liked the object to fill the frame, which resulted in a bound and taut feeling. In many of his photographs, elements are cut off on at least one side of the image. Together with the close perspective, this resulted in a confrontational immediacy that kept the viewer at bay. Renger-Patzsch combined the contour and internal lines of the buildings into subtly drawn references, an approach that was particularly appropriate for Gropius and Meyer's architecture, with its graphic surface structure, especially in the grid facade of the main building at Alfeld. The images made a theme of the geometric order and rigor of the buildings by utilizing them as the compositional backbone of the image.

Renger-Patzsch always looked at his subjects from the point of view of a visitor. No shots were taken from an elevated position or from a great distance. Hence, the series included few overall views, and where Renger-Patzsch did frame the whole complex in one image, he moved in so closely that the resulting image of the buildings was escheloned and visually foreshortened. This effect was further intensified by the portrait format of the prints. In contrast to Lill, Renger-Patzsch kept neither his distance to the architecture nor did he aim for a documentary neutrality; instead, he sought to emphasize architectonic characteristics in closeups.

This becomes especially evident in the detail shots of the main building's street elevation (number 8a; see page 40). In the detail, the photographer was able to capture the essence of the architecture. He underlined the asymmetrical design of the building, centering the image on the trussless glazed corner, and showed the stairwell and its appearance of weightlessness. At the same time, we are made aware of the clean lines in the details—the photograph invites us to count the rows of bricks and to set them into relation with the steel muntins.

Another criterion was the emphasis on dimension and room characteristics. Renger-Patzsch underscored the vague feeling of unease that a visitor may have experienced in the stairwell of the main building by selecting a vertiginous perspective straight down into the stairwell (number 10); the long corridor appeared even longer because the shot was focused on the depth of the image, leading straight into darkness (number 14).

The main compositional tools, however, were eschelons, which Renger-Patzsch preferred for machine and product feature shots; he arranged identical objects in long rows, placing them into the frame on a diagonal. This mass presentation of goods with identical form and quality personified the character of industrial production and the precision of the machine. In the now famous image of ironing tools (number 44; see page 104), Renger-Patzsch combined eschelons with a complete closeup and enlarged the objects into monumental dimensions. Despite the almost military sameness, the objects were invested with individual life through minute differences in placement, supported by the subtle focus on the quality of the material and the surface structure.

Opposite: Measuring point marking machine.

Top: Photo by Albert Renger-Patzsch, April 1928. Fagus series no. 32.

Bottom: Works photo, circa 1929.

Photograph number 16 is similarly fascinating in its ambivalence. Composed of a sequence of identical elements, the main building must be read as architecture that followed industrial production principles, underscored by the dominant use of glass and iron. An immaterial lightness was dominant. Only the two brickwork piers to the right and the left of the trussless corner referred to the structural work of the building. Again, the photographer's close standpoint to the object changed the appearance of the piers more distant from the corner; they were reduced to mere vertical strips of shadow, creating the illusion of a continuous curtain wall.

With the Fagus series, Renger-Patzsch opened a new way of looking at the architecture of the Fagus factory by interpreting its main building—which had been completed during the prewar era more than fifteen years earlier—as belonging to the International Style. Photograph number 16, at least, seemed to presume knowledge of the Bauhaus building at Dessau, completed in December of 1926—possible even communicated through the photographs by Lucia Moholy. When Renger-Patzsch's photographs were used to illustrate the Fagus factory, one was invited to look at the architecture through the aesthetic lens of the late 1920s; moreover, this was but a fragmentary view, focused only on the main building.

New Objectivity in photography should not be equated with documentary-style neutrality or even plain objectivity; instead, it was an aesthetically motivated statement on the object. In contrast to Lill, whose "shots out of the ordinary" exaggerated the factory environment through accessories and a three-dimensional context, Renger-Patzsch evoked a "pathos of beauty in machines" through his minimal and purist representation of the object and artistic composition. This, if nothing else, constituted the superior quality of the photographs in the Fagus series.

Gropius was quick to recognize not only their integrity but also the radical impact they would have on how his work was interpreted, especially in photograph number 16, which became his favorite print and nearly the only one he used of the building after 1929—to illustrate his own publications as well as features written by others on his work, as a slide for his lectures, as a large-scale print for exhibitions and again in standard format for press releases.

The modernity so exclusively expressed in the photographs by Renger-Patzsch resulted in a way of looking at Gropius that was adopted not only by the architect himself but also by all those who assessed and reviewed his work. Anything that did not suit this image of modernity was left out; no photographs illustrated commonalties with Peter Behrens's architecture, for example, and the slightly old-fashioned air of the vestibule, through which Renger-Patzsch surely passed on his tour, was obviously deemed unworthy of being photographed, as were the lesser buildings necessary to production, to list but a few of the most obvious omissions.

Thus began the fragmented view of the Fagus factory in the history of architecture—more succinctly, the focus on those building components that could be retrospectively presented as modern. By 1931, the consensus was that "the Fagus factory is the first building in the history of the new architecture that clearly expresses the new design: form following function and construction, free of decorative additions, of aesthetically driven arbitrary choices in plan and elevation."[25]

Images 8a and 16 in the Renger series, more than any others, supported the still prevailing misapprehension that the bold trussless corners and the large glass surfaces necessitated an innovative skeleton framework and that the building at Alfeld was one of the first—if not *the* first—example of a curtain wall.

From Tombstone to Villa

Tombstone, 1911–1912

Opposite: Villa Hollborn after renovation. Carl Benscheidt Sr., private residence. Factory photo, 1930s.

Walter Gropius and Adolf Meyer were not only the architects of the Fagus factory, they also handled many private commissions for the Benscheidt family. These were projects of a representational nature—that is, intended to demonstrate the family's modern attitude and its prominent position in society. The earliest example of this kind of representational work was from 1911–1912: the family tombstone for Alfeld's Neuer Friedhof (new cemetery). Having the company architect design one's family headstone had become de rigueur among those who had the means to do so and the Benscheidts were following the example of many well-to-do entrepreneurs of their day.

Carl Benscheidt's youngest child, Fritz Benscheidt, died on July 1, 1911. Gropius and Meyer probably designed the headstone during the second half of the same year.[1] A vertical stone slab was placed at the center of the wide plot, with pylons on either side. The simple slab was decorated with the image of a burning oil lamp set in a circle in relief and the name Benscheidt carved into the stone below. The names and dates of the family members buried in the grave were carved into low walls that reached out from the pylons on either side and framed the rectangular plot with volutes at the ends of the base.

Benscheidt family grave.

It is surprising to see how closely the design of the headstone relates to the architecture the team was creating at the same time. The escarped pylons, more than any other element, are reminiscent of the stairwells in the main building at Fagus; as to the preliminary project from April 1911, a comparison to the details of the roof surround almost imposes itself. Why the architectonic developed for buildings—compact contour and steep angles that evoke authority and monumentality—was applied to a tombstone that was no more than 160 centimeters high can be explained by its pathos of forms. On the other hand, Gropius and Meyer's work steered away from unwarranted exaggeration or disproportionate size. The restrained simplicity of the tombstone succeeded through harmonious proportions and a grave and dignified manner.

Renovation and Interior: Benscheidt Jr.'s Private Home, 1923–1926

Having one's private villa designed by the company architect had also become a tradition among factory owners, but for Karl Benscheidt Jr., who lived with his family in the parental home of his wife, a new villa was outside of the range of possibilities. Instead, he chose to renovate the home in several stages between 1923 and 1926. It had been built for his father-in-law, music director Robert Linnarz, in 1898–1899 at 13 Kaiser-Wilhelm-Strasse in Alfeld. Benscheidt commissioned Gropius and his office to renovate room by room.

The work began in 1923 with the kitchen, where a new floor was laid and new tiling installed on the walls up to the height of the doors.[2] The architects kept the renovation to a minimum due to the currency devalutation: doorframes and panels were simply refinished; the old fixtures were preserved and exchanged for Gropius door-handles at a much later date. The kitchen was appointed in simple white lacquered furnishings with a clear finish on all seat and work surfaces. The recessed bases and the spherical handles stood out in contrasting black. One notable detail was the front chair legs, which were set on a bias. These pieces were probably made in Alfeld after plans drafted at Weimar.

Both the sideboard and the cabinet had the characteristic features of the furniture that Gropius and Meyer designed for dining and sitting room suites before World War I. A

Karl Benscheidt Jr.'s home. Kitchen. Photo by Edmund Lill, first half of 1923.

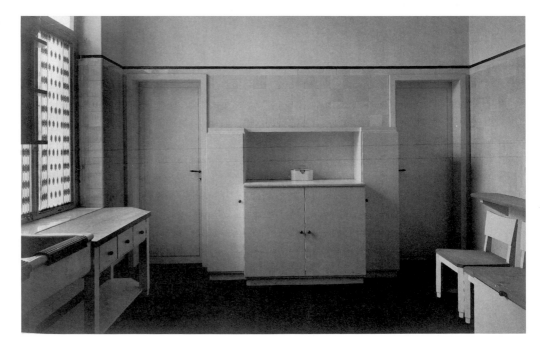

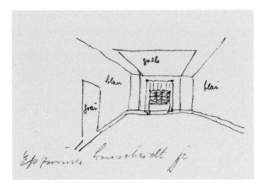

dominant feature was the architectonic character of the upright furniture and another the rounded or beveled edges and overhanging shelves. Overall, the pieces had a stocky weightiness, similar to Neufert's furniture for the company apartment in the building Am Weidenknick.[3]

Probably as early as December 1923, the dining room and the living room were repainted by the Bauhaus mural workshop.[4] No new furniture was designed for these rooms. However, Gropius's estate contains a sheet labeled "dining room for C. Benscheidt Jr." that features color and fabric samples as well as a small interior perspective drawing of the room. The unsigned and undated sketch shows blue walls with a field of yellow around the window and a ceiling mirror reflecting light into the room. The doors and baseboards are painted in gray. A light, natural white gauze was chosen for the net curtains, with the outer curtain in strong brick red.

From May and June 1924 there are drawings for the renovation of the entrance area with outdoor steps as well as an overhanging sheltering roof above the front door, a vestibule, stairwell, corridor, restroom, and a master study. But application to the building authorities was not made until a year later, at the end of August 1925. Limestone slabs from Solnhofen were chosen for the vestibule floor and combined with black glass on the walls up to 130 centimeters. Large plate-glass surfaces in the entrance doors and frosted glass doors to the living room and dining room allowed natural light to pour into the hallway, which was also equipped with a number of cubic lighting fixtures in frosted glass set in thin nickel frames, some recessed in the wall and others in the ceiling. Practical closets with sliding doors enhanced the modern character of the space.

The renovation work was completed shortly before Christmas 1925; the furniture for the master study was, however, only drafted. Throughout 1926, the pieces were delivered one by one: a black book-

Karl Benscheidt Jr.'s home. Ground-floor hallway, 1980s.

case for the full 5.5-meter width of the room, four easy chairs set on spherical feet, a low table, a rectangular table painted black, and a ceiling light fixture made of two sheets of glass attached one atop the other. The bookcase and the leather chairs especially were ponderous yet understated in shape and again reminiscent of the furniture Gropius and Meyer had designed in the prewar years.

The plain radio cabinet for the music room (living room) was finished in black paint and much more modern in character. This cabinet, now part of the Bauhaus collection at the Weimar Art Museum, the bookcase in the study, and the built-in wardrobes in the hall were all built by Dessau carpenter G. Lautenbach.[5] Among the more interesting pieces of furniture in Benscheidt's house were the furnishings in the guest room on the second floor: a cubic night table in white finish and a washstand—both since purchased by the Weimar Art Museum—and a group of four upholstered chairs around a square table. Based on their style, these pieces can be dated to circa 1923–1924; today, the latter are displayed in the museum of the Fagus factory.[6]

The house for Benscheidt Jr. was the most extensive interior design project Gropius worked on in collaboration with Meyer during the Bauhaus years.

Villa Projects for Benscheidt Sr., 1925–1926

Benscheidt Sr. lived in a rented apartment near the factory and had thought about building a customized home for some time. The Fagus archives contain a plan, dated July 1, 1923, and headed "Modified project for a new villa. Fagus factory Karl Benscheidt." The architecture in this plan is conventional and prewar in style. The fact that the plan was drafted by an employee at Fagus leads one to assume that Benscheidt Sr. may have intended to cut costs by readying the plan in-house and asking an outside expert to upgrade and customize it later.

Karl Benscheidt Jr.'s home. Chairs and table for guest room.

The project was probably put on hold because of the currency devaluation. Still, it is surprising that Benscheidt Sr. would have hesitated to involve Gropius and Meyer, whose designs for residential homes had caused a stir ever since 1921. Benscheidt's attitude is explained in his correspondence where he frequently expresses his dissatisfaction with the project management, the lack of supervision at the construction site, and his displeasure at the high fees. Since founding the Bauhaus, Gropius no longer handled the correspondence for his practice personally, nor did he come to Alfeld very often. Adolf Meyer, too, overworked in his dual roles of studio manager and teacher of architecture at the Bauhaus, was rarely on site. Gropius inter-

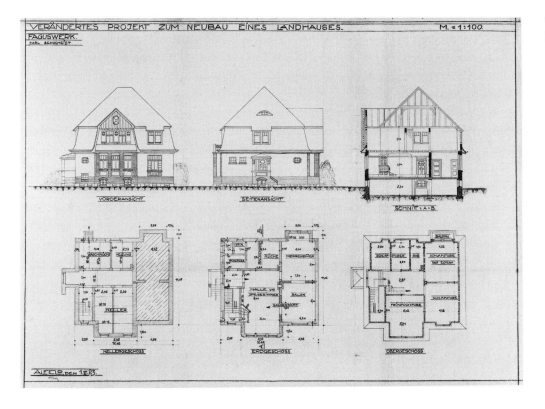

vened only when difficult situations arose. Otherwise, he simply wrote the invoices. All decisions were handled by telephone.

In 1924, matters came to a head. When Benscheidt complained about the slow, often complicated, and, hence, expensive manner in which the office handled commissions, Gropius replied: "It is natural that a way of working that is setting a new path in the area of building requires different preliminary work and trials than the usual old hat, which focuses only on speed and cost efficiency. I think you can be content with the factory we have built for you, as it has become famous nationally and internationally as an exemplary factory. To achieve this was possible only with the kind of intensive attention I and my team have given your project. The best is an enemy of the average good and you can't force good ideas to be ready for delivery on any particular day."7

One should note that Benscheidt Sr. worked with the architect W. Rudolph since 1922. Rudolph was responsible not only for the design of the employee housing Am Weidenknick but also for refurbishing several buildings into workers' apartments. This decision must have been difficult to bear for Gropius, who had tried since 1911 to convince Benscheidt Sr. that he should build a workers' settlement based on his plans for the Janikow estate in 1909. But the client seems to have wanted an architect who would be available on site, who would give personal attention to the project, who would work efficiently, and whose invoices would be reasonable.

For Gropius and his practice, one result of this confrontation was that on-site management was transferred to Ernst Neufert, who moved to Alfeld in 1923. For better communication, Neufert clarified what needed to be done on site and passed this information on to Weimar—if necessary, accompanied by sketches. Gropius's team then completed plans and Neufert ensured that they were carried out and implemented in Alfeld.

In contrast to his son, who embraced modernism wholeheartedly, Benscheidt Sr. seems to have accepted the enervating and expensive collaboration with Gropius and Meyer first and foremost as a price to pay for good advertising for his factory. Nevertheless, in the 1920s he did commission Gropius to design some private projects and this indicates that he, too, was quite open to avant-garde ideas. The neo-Biedermeier style in the anonymous plan for a villa from 1923 would not have worked on the property chosen near the Fagus factory in 1925. For architectural continuity alone, there was no alternative to Gropius and Meyer, even though they were difficult to work with. The decision to ask another architect to draft a plan for the house may have been simply a means of obtaining an alternative model that Benscheidt could hold up in negotiations as a counterargument.

For the moment, however, all plans for a villa were put aside. Instead, Benscheidt Sr. commissioned Gropius's office to design a new living room set. He was dissatisfied with the sketches sent to him (which have, unfortunately, not been preserved) and asked for new drawings to be made. The only items that were executed, in the end, were a leather sofa, a leather armchair, and a round oak table. The pieces were executed in the early fall of 1925.[8] Benscheidt Sr. ordered three table lamps from the metal workshop at the Bauhaus, probably the model known as the Bauhaus lamp, designed by Karl Jucker and Wilhelm Wagenfeld.[9] The Bauhaus also delivered a tablecloth and a cushion cover for the master study.

Plans for Carl Benscheidt Sr.'s villa. Design by Carl Fieger, 1925.

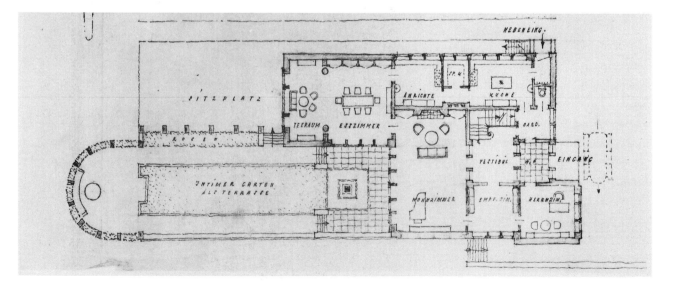

Early in 1925, Carl Benscheidt Sr. decided to ask Gropius and his team to build a villa on his property near the Fagus complex. Throughout February and March, Adolf Meyer, Ernst Neufert, and Karl Fieger worked on plans for the project.[10] Karl Fieger's estate papers include a floor plan that may represent this phase of the planning process. It is unclear, however, whether the drawings, signed by Fieger, were studio drafts or Fieger's own submissions. The latter seems more likely.[11]

The design envisioned a two-story building in *L*-formation with a flat roof. The generous living area was the core of the house, consisting of a music room, a dining room, and a tea room, arranged on two sides of a small courtyard (complete with outdoor sculpture). The exterior was reminiscent of J.J.P. Oud's design for the Kallenbach house in Berlin (1921), especially in the near floor-height windows divided only by narrow posts and connected by a continuous cantilevered concrete roof. All these components, as well as the small courtyard at the center, also featured in the earlier design by Oud.

At the beginning of April 1925, Benscheidt Sr. informed Gropius that he now wanted to build the villa on the Wahrberg hillside overlooking the Fagus factory site. Benscheidt owned a large property here, which included a gravel pit and an orchard on the crest of the hill. This was to be the site for Benscheidt's villa with a view down onto the Fagus factory, a classic setup for a factory owner and entrepreneur. A new access road would be necessary and the plan foresaw a serpentine road up the hill; the total building costs were accordingly high, estimated at a staggering 150,000 marks. Some of the correspondence dealing with this project is preserved. From these letters, it appears that Gropius and the other members of his office prepared three different designs for this planning phase, even though the drawings no longer exist. However, several site plans for the road (June 1925) show at least the outline of the house and its garden setting in all three versions.

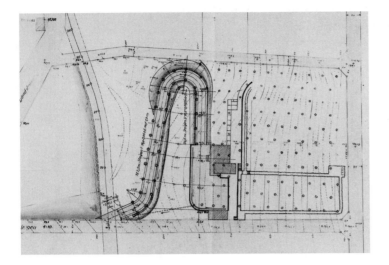

Carl Benscheidt Sr.'s villa. Site plan variation, June 1925.

The most interesting version featured an oblong main fabric, with a taller cuboid at a right angle and extending beyond the main fabric to the rear. It is reasonable to assume that the house would have been topped by a flat roof, part of which would probably have been a roof patio. In principle, the plan had much in common with Gropius's own residence in Dessau, in the planning process at the same time. The two other drafts for the Benscheidt villa showed a plain rectangle and a design with a square ground plan, respectively. The latter was of a fortress-like character set on an artificial plateau. Located right above the gravel pit, this would undoubtedly have created an imposing backdrop for the house.

Benscheidt was repeatedly dissatisfied with the manner in which Gropius worked, such as changing the floor plan without consulting the client or considering his wishes. Moreover, Benscheidt felt that the efforts undertaken to create so many preliminary variations were a means of increasing the cost. Gropius replied: "You wrote that it is unnecessary to draw elevations of the exterior until we are fully agreed on the ground and floor plans. It would indeed by irresponsible on the part of any architect to design a ground plan without an elevation. A house is an organism; the ground plan is but a projection of the whole fabric. That is why the preliminary work is so complex—because each ground plan must be considered in all three dimensions.[12]"

By November 1925, the finished plan was ready at the office, requiring only Benscheidt's final approval. To this end, Gropius invited Benscheidt and his wife to Dessau to show them the Bauhaus master's houses, then under construction, and the house of the Bauhaus director—a preview of what their own villa would look like. But Benscheidt was elected chairman of a creditors group and could not take the time to go. At the same time, he began to express doubts that he would be able to build after all because of the economic situation.

Finally, a meeting took place in Alfeld at the beginning of December 1925, and several small changes were discussed. Preliminary cost estimates began to arrive from various suppliers, from which we can determine that the house was to be constructed in faced brickwork, probably in the same leather-yellow bricks as the Fagus factory, to create a visual link between villa and factory.[13]

In June 1926, Benscheidt reported that he did not have sufficient funds at the moment, but felt confident that his cashflow would soon improve. Still, the project would have to be more modest in scale. The total cost for the villa was reduced to 120,000 marks, still an impressive amount of money. Benscheidt attended the inauguration of the Bauhaus building in Dessau on December 6, 1926, and some other details were clarified. In time for Christmas, Benscheidt received a set of three fully detailed plans for each variation, of which none have been preserved. The couple spent the holidays studying each plan in turn. They complained that, once again, Gropius had made alterations in areas that had already been agreed upon. By the end of February 1927, Benscheidt Sr. asked Gropius to release him from the contract, as financial circumstances no longer made it possible to build the house. Neither party would return to the plans for a villa for Benscheidt Sr.

Villa Hollborn Renovation, 1927–1928

Still in the same year, Carl Benscheidt Sr. decided to renovate the villa Hollborn, his property since 1922 and leased to Fagus employees, and take it as his residence. The contract was not offered to Gropius's practice, however, but directly to Ernst Neufert. Apparently, Benscheidt was so dissatisfied with Gropius's lack of cooperation that he preferred to retain the former studio manager instead. The young professor from the Staatliche Bauhochschule in Weimar was eager for contracts and his pragmatic efficiency, of which the client was well aware, promised quick decisions, smooth collaboration, and on-time completion.

The late-nineteenth-century villa was located on a secluded property at some distance from the Fagus factory. Neufert undertook few changes to the exterior: outdoor steps and a vestibule at the main entrance, a glass verandah with access to the garden at the rear, a balcony, and new windows. Even these changes were so restrained, from an architectural standpoint, that they barely influenced the character of the house. Unfortunately, there is very little information about the interior design: all we know is that interior doors were made of exotic wood and that built-in closets were installed. After less than a year of renovation work, the house was ready for occupation by the end of 1928. The furniture for the dining room, the bedroom, and the guest room, designed by Neufert and executed by a carpenter in the town of Münder near Hanover, was also delivered on schedule.[14]

Villa Hollborn after renovation. Carl Benscheidt Sr.'s home. Garden side. Factory photo, 1930s.

Maintaining Fagus

Jürgen Götz

Construction and Maintenance: An Overview

The Fagus factory has never been easy to maintain. This is eloquently documented in a paper headed "Structural Maintenance," found in the account book at Gropius's office. The document contains a list of amounts invoiced in the mid-1920s; a mere fifteen years after completion, the buildings were already in need of repair under the architect's supervision.

Benscheidt Sr. and Jr. were as diligent in looking after the physical structure of their factory as they were in conducting their business. For a short period, from 1939 to 1945, they were unable to maintain this high standard, but the buildings and the machinery survived the war undamaged. In fact, the complex was in such good condition that it was declared a protected heritage site in 1946 to prevent dismantling. This may have been first instance in Germany where a building in the style of the early modern movement was officially designated for conservation, though not necessarily in the full sense of "heritage" as it was then understood. Aware of the historic significance of his building, now famous worldwide through Nikolaus Pevsner's slim volume *Pioneers of the Modern Movement*, Karl Benscheidt began to renovate the factory buildings after World War II. When Walter Gropius stopped by for a visit in 1951 on his second trip to Germany after 1945, he found the complex in excellent condition.

The economic miracle of the 1950s had made such efforts financially feasible. As the economy slowed in the decade that followed, less money was available and necessary measures were put on hold. By the 1970s, it was evident that several areas were in desperate need of repair, although the damage was not very visible on the outside, with the exception of the large rust spots on the steel plates in the window frames. To visitors, the factory still showed a very presentable face. The damage on the roofs, the cracks in the wall just below the roofline, and the plaster damage on the warehouse—all these were barely noticeable to the naked eye.

Since the very beginning of production, visitors were always welcome. Those now coming with a background in the history of architecture invariably noticed the glazing as the outstanding design characteristic. Art history had contributed to this view of the building complex. The somewhat myopic focus on the main building—and, more specifically, on the glazing—helped shape the public perception that restoring the factory complex was synonymous

Oppostie: Main building during renovation, 1990.

with restoring the glazing. This has meant that many other factors, presented on the following pages, have been neglected.

Esthetically, the individual structures of the Fagus complex (the main building, the production hall, the drying kilns, the warehouse, and the sawmill) were conceived as independent units; structurally, however, they were all interconnected. Thus, the rear wall of the main building carried the load of the floor joists and the trusses of the strutted frame of the production hall on its far side. The corbels were, in fact, the extensions of the floor beams that pierced the wall. The same support system was used on the side of the drying kilns. Problems in structural stability resulted from this design and manifested themselves in kinetic chains that lacked a mathematical or static resolution. In other words, the design resulted in a building without true structural stability. Individual shear walls were added for reinforcement, but this method proved insufficient. The formation of partial kinetic chains weakened the structure and ultimately led to very real damage due to excessive deformation.

The main building was erected on top of a structurally stable basement with flat caps. Nonreinforced (or compressed) concrete, mixed with pebble dashing, was used for the basement walls, an unfortunate blend unable to support great individual loads. From the basement upward, the building rose in plain brickwork with reinforced wood floors. The ceilings were underpinned with a formwork shell and finished in rough-cast plaster on the services installation side. The floors were composed of planks on loose sleepers—that is, sleepers that were not fixed between the floor joists. Hence, the ceilings in the main building were not continuous shears and thus were unable to fulfill the necessary bracing function.

Had the concrete ceiling just below the roof, drafted in the original plan, been installed, the construction, on the whole, would have worked quite well. However, this was never executed in either of the two construction phases. Between the third-floor ceiling and the roof a large hollow cavity remained, permeable to wind and tending to excessive condensation, which damaged the building below, especially in the area of the main staircase and its two cantilevered corners. The roof envelope, turned brittle with the passage of time, and the permeable inner roof vents exacerbated the damage.

In keeping with the practice of the time, the parapet floor of the main building had neither joints and nor insulation. The southeast side of the building, measuring 46.5 meters, was

Schematic of main building structure.

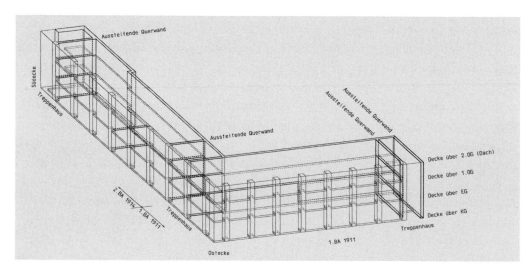

too long for this kind of construction. Hence, extensions were used on the inside; this led to cracks in their brick covering and to joint erosion, allowing rainwater to seep in. The girders began to rust fairly quickly, accelerating the overall deterioration process.

The foundation around the building posts in the main building were overstressed. The ground beneath began to settle and many cracks appeared in the parapet brickwork. Moreover, the high groundwater level near the Leine River transmitted the shocks from the nearby north-south railroad line. Until the 1960s, the railroad ties were loose—that is, they were not welded; this meant that the shock and vibration from the ties and the many shunting points at Alfeld's train station had a direct impact on the building. Between 1961 and 1964, the ties were welded and the situation improved considerably, not least because rail traffic in general calmed down and a new ICE (rapid intercity train) route was installed further east of Alfeld and the factory complex.

The other buildings in the complex were structurally much simpler. Thus, the drying shed was a simple brickwork structure with an intermediate ceiling and a platform roof; the main production hall had a timberwork roof, with a strut frame and skylights, resting on cast-iron posts. The tool-and-die shop, too, was conventional in construction: a pure brickwork structure with strutted roof frame. The coal and wood shavings bunker was built in the same manner, with the addition of a concrete extension topped by a massive platform roof to provide storage space for the combustibles. The boiler and machine house differed in that it was a combination of steel post-and-beam and brickwork dissolving into large windows in the machine house.

The warehouse was the largest building of the complex in terms of cubic volume. This was a relatively complicated multistory post-and-beam structure on a brickwork base, where the rough lasts were stored to dry, sometimes for several years. It was designed to absorb the weight of the millions of lasts stacked up to a height of 15 meters. The warehouse interior was fully sealed against incident daylight and yet well ventilated and able to evacuate the moisture from drying wood. On the outside, the warehouse was finished in rough-cast plaster and pebble dashing and structured with horizontal grooves.

The windows of the main building were the trademark feature of the Fagus factory and have been written about frequently since the late 1920s. The window openings were intrados frames composed of L beams; the internal membering with horizontal and vertical muntins was differentiated in that all the verticals appeared more slender from the outside, while the horizontals appeared wider. These frames were, however, only floor-to-floor height, screwed to the building on four sides; one string course that reached across three floors consisted, in fact, of three different sections. Along the sides of the building, 3-millimeter-thick steel plates sealed the wedge between window frame and piers. The glazing was 45-millimeter-thick building glass inserted into a thick putty rebate.

The windows from the construction phases were treated differently, from a structural perspective. In the first building phase, the frames were commercial T and I beams, riveted or bolted together. The vertical muntins, consisting of I beams, were bolted to the frame, and the horizontals, consisting of T profiles, were simply inserted through the rib of the vertical beam. Additional fasteners for the bottom-hinged sash windows, installed in a checkerboard pattern for ventilation, as well as other fasteners for the steel plates in the parapet and ceiling areas, held the horizontal muntins firmly in place. The result was a relatively stable construction, albeit not a very differentiated design.

The windows for the first construction phase were manufactured by a Berlin iron and steel construction firm; for the second phase, windows were delivered by Fenestra, a company that specialized in this type of glazing. Based in Düsseldorf, Fenestra had been manufacturing windows for several decades using special profiles that were rolled out to specification off-site. The windows they manufactured were much slimmer in profile and very popular in the 1920s. Several Mies van der Rohe buildings from that era featured Fenestra glazing. In the Fagus buildings, the horizontal muntins were formed by two interlocking U-beams into which the vertical muntins, whose narrow look was enhanced by concave molding on both sides, were inserted through a slot and then clenched. Four central, vertically pivoted sash windows provided ventilation. This modification to the approach used in the first construction phase created an elegant design based on the difference in width between horizontal and vertical muntins and the proportional harmony of the vertically pivoted sash windows to the structure as a whole. But altogether, the second construction turned out to be less stable. The static strength was too low in both constructions. This was especially true for the south corner without piers.

The main production hall, the boiler and power house, and the track scale building featured cast-iron window frames, riveted and bolted together from commercial iron beams by Wesselmann, a company very near the Fagus factory. Despite their size, these relatively simple windows have stayed in good condition over the years, as iron is much less susceptible to corrosion than steel.

Problems arose from the very beginning with the string-coursed windows. Even photographs taken prior to 1919 reveal the first traces of rust; a rust-proof coating applied in 1923 turned out to be inadequate and had to be renewed in the following year. By 1931, the problems were severe and Karl Benscheidt had to report to Gropius's practice: "The steel window frames of my main building are all rusty now. It is especially noticeable on all riveted seams. The worst area is the new staircase, where the clock is. I planned to have the window frames in the stairwell painted from the inside. In doing so, we realized that some areas are so badly rusted that the entire window frame would need to be taken out and disassembled to remove the rust. Some of the steel plates have to be removed altogether because they are rusted right through. I have contacted Fenestra-Crittal . . . and have received a letter from them . . . I am very surprised that after such a [short] time, the company seems to think it necessary and advisable to replace the windows altogether. I feel that fifteen years is not a very long time. As far as I am concerned, they should last at least twice as long."

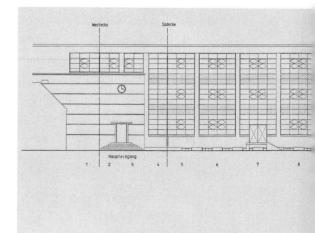

Gropius intervened with the supplier in Düsseldorf, although no documentation exists of the exchange. It is remarkable, however, that, even at this early date, the same problems that would plague the building later on were discussed, as were the effort and expense required to fix them. Moreover, the manufacturer declared quite openly that the serviceable life of his product was limited.

We now know that both facade systems in the main building were treated with rust removal and protective coatings. Individual muntins, possibly even whole sections of the facades, were replaced in the early years. More specifically, damage occurred in the following areas:

- The older window construction by Hirsch turned out to be quite solid overall, yet, even with the best care, it was very susceptible to corrosion at the crossing points between vertical and horizontal muntins. The sections near the ceilings were not only connected to the solid ceiling that projected between the battered piers but also they were bolted together and were subject to particular stresses. As a result, the individual parts warped drastically. Gaps inevitably formed, followed by rust, the corrosion being so severe that even some of the thicker profiles rusted right through. Even the U beams that framed the compressed concrete slabs projecting between the piers were subject to corrosion.
- The Fenestra products were manufactured in less solid dimensions. Installed on the southeast and southwest sides of the main building, they were particularly exposed to wind, sun, and pelting rain, reducing their serviceable life. Moreover, the building tended to be drafty to begin with and this exacerbated the problems; the high suction pressure of the shavings exhaust created a negative pressure in the main production hall that was transferred onto the facade every time the door to the main building was opened. Independent statements by former employees confirm that the facade would literally buckle inward when this happened. Conversely, whenever a door slammed shut because of the strong draft, the facade would bulge visibly outward. The result was considerable friction at the squash points in the vertical muntins, abrading the rustproof coating and allowing water seepage. In combination with the moisture from condensation, the nonventilated profiles also corroded on the inside. In some instances, the corrosion was so extreme that the muntins rusted right through. Prior to renovation, some windows were literally held together by putty. The frames around the pivoted sash windows rusted so badly that they could no longer be opened or closed, which increased the draft even further.

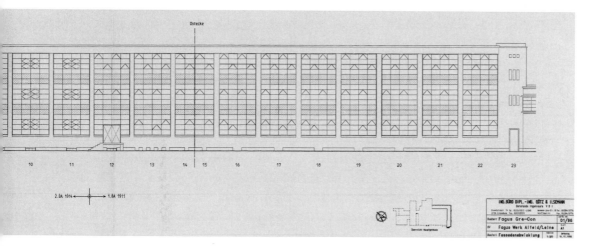

Developed view of main building facades.

- The draftiness and natural wind pressure on the windows combined with the slumping of the projecting solid ceilings may have caused many of the facade components to warp outward, like a sack of potatoes; this was especially noticeable in the lower section of the building, where the warping extended, in some instances, all the way to the frame profile. These distortions were visible signs of the excessive stresses brought to bear on the window components.

- The glazing of the staircases posed a unique set of problems; here, there were no solid ceilings to which individual panels could be bolted, thereby creating a continuous vertical band consisting of three window elements. This is unnoticeable from the outside, because the overall patterns of openings and steel plates was maintained across three floors. During the first construction phase of the staircase, an attempt was made to brace the vertical muntins by bolting steel beams to them from the inside. This proved an effective solution and has lasted into the present. The main staircase, on the other hand, presented an altogether different scenario; it required installing the glazing around the south corner without any visible supports. By orientation alone, this corner was particularly exposed to the elements. Yet, in contrast to the construction of the first staircase, no additional measures were taken to brace or strengthen the structure, and sections of this facade have been subject to extreme deformation leading to the damage described above. Unfortunately, no documentation exists about efforts taken at the time to rectify the problem. In any case, regardless of specifics, any efforts undertaken were obviously unsuccessful even then, because former Fagus employees remember that this corner had to be rebuilt in the 1950s. In the absence of records, we can no longer reconstruct how extensive the renovation was, but the pivoting sash windows, originally installed level with the landings, are no longer in place today.

- In the power house, too, many components of the facade were taken out and replaced. For a recent renovation project, photographs taken many years ago were studied and proved that the facade no longer resembled the one that had been originally installed. Photographs and the presence of connectors to the large cast-iron window frames of the boiler house point to the fact that an iron frame facade had been installed in this building during World War I. We do not know when this change—visible still today at the corner posts of the building—actually took place. Former employees cannot remember a renovation so extensive as to include such a drastic replacement.

- When the rustproof paint was removed from the second-floor section of row 17 for exhibition purposes in 1994, it was immediately apparent how much the original window construction had been changed through various repair measures over time. With the protective coating removed, different types of steel were uncovered, indicating that beams had been replaced; additional rivets and bolts were also revealed, obviously intended to strengthen the facade around the openable components. The lower L profile of the frame may have rusted right through and was probably exchanged for a smaller profile. It is impossible, at this time, to determine when this exchange, or the installation of new sheet-plate panels, may have taken place. The new joints were spot welded. Was the entire section of windows removed for these repairs? Just how extensive was the renovation? Or was this an isolated incident? These and other questions are unanswerable because of a lack of documents. But documentation aside, we do know that the facade required heavy maintenance and repair from the very beginning.

By the early 1980s, the damage had become so severe that immediate action was necessary. At the outset, an engineering firm from Hildesheim confirmed that the crack formation had stabilized. Hence, the foundation did not have to be strengthened, but the state of the main building was the greatest concern and this is where the renovation began. Everyone agreed on how to tackle the roof repair, which would go hand in hand with the installation of the inserted ceiling that would brace the fabric of the main building (as had been envisioned in the original plan, but never executed). This was a vital prerequisite to further repair of the window components. Because each window frame was bolted to the building on four sides, deformations in the structure affected the glazing. The average breakage rate was forty windowpanes per year.

In 1984–1985, heated discussions began on whether to repair or replace window components, a discussion that continues even today. The issue is a contentious one because academic ideas on the ideal maintenance of an internationally famous historic site collide with the practical aspect of building preservation and ensuring that the production processes, unchanged over the course of seventy-five years, could continue unimpeded, thus preserving not only a building but also a rare continuity in manufacturing. Traditionalists in conservation felt that it would and should be possible to reinstall the original windows. An analysis revealed, however, that many components were too weak to be reused. The question of whether or not these were, in fact, original components did not arise, as no one had considered the problem from this perspective. The repairs and renovations in the complex during the early years had been so carefully executed that they were rarely visible at first glance.

As investigations continued, the current occupants joined in requesting that the working conditions in the office areas be improved; workstations anywhere near the windows were notorious among the staff because of draft and extreme heat or cold, depending upon the season. Office workers stationed in some of these areas were known to wear hats, scarves, and long underwear in winter. These conditions made a mockery of the architect's intentions. They certainly fell far short of the ideal "dignity of the unified great idea that is the driving force behind everything," as Gropius had called it in 1911.

Although an air conditioner had been installed, comfort levels during the summer months were still unsatisfactory. Comfort was also insufficient in winter; last production had switched from wood to plastics and thus wood remnants were no longer available for heating and the oil used instead was expensive. Moreover, the management wished to maintain the original distribution of usage, modifying production and operating processes only when it was absolutely necessary. Any discussions about changes in use were therefore unproductive.

All these factors pointed to insulated glazing as the best option for repair. To satisfy conservation requirements, however, the insulated glazing would have to meet the following standards in structural and visual design:

- Use steel for the window construction.
- Maintain the difference in style for the two facade sections.
- Accept scale changes only on the interior.
- Ensure that the different esthetics of the two facade sections remains clear.
- The number, placement, and function of the ventilation components should remain unaltered.

- The new glazing should approximate the original glass as much as possible in terms of color and reflection.
- The new protective coating for the steel profiles should replicate the original coating as much as possible.

The first renovation plan was developed in 1985 by Professor Jörn Behnsen, an architect consulted on behalf of the conservation authorities. This plan maintained the differentiated formal language in the two building sections and the dimensions of the muntins on the exterior, increasing the thickness of the muntins only on the inside for greater structural stability. The plan did envision replacing all window components. The conservation authorities, however, preferred to keep existing components.

In the interest of objectivity and because the discussion surrounding the renovation of this important historical edifice had caught the public's attention, in September 1985 the current owners and the conservation authorities invited conservation experts, historians of architecture, and journalists to a forum in Alfeld where they could exchange ideas and discuss conservation options. All agreed that original window components should be preserved and reinstalled whenever possible. Where new glazing was necessary, it should replicate the original as much as possible. Other options—for example, a second glass skin behind the original facade (box-window principle)—were rejected because they would have fundamentally changed the look of the building. To investigate all possible avenues for repair, consultants were asked to prepare an expert report on whether or not the old types of steel could be welded. They concluded that this would not be possible in all cases. Moreover, in order to reuse partial sections from facade components damaged beyond repair and join them with new components, special procedures would be required.

The factory owners had initially agreed to reuse old window components only in the staircases. As negotiations continued, all parties agreed that such components could also be reinstalled in the conference rooms on the east corner, as these areas were used only intermittently. This compromise has meant that fields 1–5 and 12–16 have been preserved in their original form. Despite good intentions, a complete section dating from the second construction phase could not be accomplished, however, because the entire southeast side between the two stairwells is assigned to office use and consideration had to be given to the poor condition of the steel of these components. Behnsen altered the plan so that the new components would match the old windows in all external details. New solutions were sought, however, for the structural problems—these were different in each building section—and to meet user requirements.

From September 1986 onward, the components were taken out and replaced with new or restored panes. Naturally, this was a gradual process of removing and replacing the sections row by row, with the last one, the glazing in the main stairwell, coming in 1990. The type of glass used for the insulated glazing was so similar to the original panes that when five of them were installed on a trial basis, experts were unable to tell the new from the old.

But this was only the beginning in terms of renovating the entire complex. While the last sections of glazing were still being installed, work began on the chimney, which was rebuilt to its previous height and topped with the original cowl. Next, the main production hall had to be renovated, a step-by-step process to ensure uninterrupted production. The cast-iron window frames and the strutted frame construction (weakened by fungus) were repaired or replaced.

Preserving the boiler and machine house was less challenging, from a technical point of view. However, when older photographs were compared with more recent ones, it became evident that the large facade components had already been replaced or restored. The main issue was how to determine which sections were new (or newer) and what parts of the building may have looked like originally. In many cases, there were no plans or drafts from Gropius's practice and alterations made during the initial construction or at a later date were not documented. Overall, the issue was difficult to resolve and constant communication was necessary with the conservators to ensure a mutually satisfactory result.

The final task, remodeling the warehouse, is currently underway in preparation for Expo 2000. Efforts continue to find solutions for this structure commensurate with a heritage site of such caliber. This building has been the least appreciated section of the complex, yet it is vitally important to the entire complex—not only in production but also in aesthetic terms.

With the best of intentions, a project of this scale and duration is bound to encounter difficulties and even conflict, as the interests of owners, architects, and conservationists are often divergent. Looking at the press coverage of the work on the main building, for example, it is evident that the articles were unable to convey the true intentions of either the conservation authorities or the factory owners. Often the tone is academic, conservative, and critical, defending the reinstallation of the original glazing components as the only acceptable path, with no recognition or acknowledgment of how this might usefully be accomplished.

Such media coverage was hardly intended to promote true dialogue. Instead, it seemed to speak for the creation of a Fagus-Werk museum. But this factory is neither church nor castle put to limited use under modest requirements for comfort. On the contrary. This is an active production site where the funds that are put into renovation and building projects must be earned in a very direct and real manner. Fagus is still the mid-sized family-run operation it has always been and the same product is being manufactured in the same rooms—a circumstance as unusual as it is rare in today's manufacturing world.

The subsidies provided by the government of Lower Saxony, the Federal Republic of Germany, the European Union, and, more recently, the German Foundation for the Protection of Monuments have been granted not only because of the incontestable international significance of the complex but also because of this very continuity in the use of the site. All have contributed to the conservation concepts. The key to ensuring the continued production of shoe lasts in the main production hall is flexibility. And flexibility translates into a more liberal approach that may consequently reduce friction between all concerned parties. Yet bringing competing interests into harmony forms a big part of any ambitious renovation project, and meaningful solutions must be found. The reaction of architecture enthusiasts who have come to the site from around the world has been unfailingly positive. This alone, if nothing else, is proof that meaningful solutions have indeed been found.

Notes

1   On Rikli, see Giedion 1982, pp. 723–727.

2   Carl Benscheidt Sr. 1947, p. 116. Also contains the following description: "In the shop window I would display drawings of crippled feet mounted on a red background and accompanied by letters of gratitude. This display caused such a stir that crowds of curious onlookers were drawn to it for months on end."

3   See Krabbe 1974, p. 83, ftn. 308: "Proponents of traditional medicine generally criticized the sheer volume of advertising practiced by naturopaths (in the form of advertisements and brochures, often publishing letters of gratitude from patients whose supposedly incurable disease had been cured), accusing them of undisguised manipulation."

4   Carl Benscheidt Sr., 1947, p. 177. See also Nelson 1975, p. 13.

5   Eine Heimstätte deutscher Industrie. In *Der Schuhmarkt* 1899, No.13 (31.3.), p. 49.

6   C. Benscheidt Sr., 1947, p. 299. He felt that the remark on cowardice was a "slap in the face."

7   C. Benscheidt Sr., 1947, p. 302.

8   Last (for shoe last) + co[mpany].

9   Scene from the London Fair. Fine Exhibit of C. Behrens' Alfeld Last Works, Germany. In: *Superintendent and Foreman* 65. 1912, No. 13 (25.12), pp. 51–54; 54.

10   C. Benscheidt Sr., 1947, p. 316.

11   C. Benscheidt Sr., 1947, p. 321, specific reference to this circumstance.

12   I am grateful to Helmut Knocke, Stadtarchiv Hanover, for research on the biographical data and professional stages of Eduard Werner.

13   C. Benscheidt Sr., 1947, p. 173, *Denkmaltopographie Niedersachsen, Stadt Hanover*, Vol. 2 (Brunswick 1985), pp. 144f.

14   The Fagus archives contain drawings for all these housing estates. On Körtingsdorf, see W. Buschmann: *Linden. Geschichte einer Industriestadt im 19.*

Jahrhundert (Hildesheim 1981), pp. 379–387.

15   C. Benscheidt Sr. 1947, pp. 173f.

16   C. Benscheidt Sr. 1947, p. 321.

17   C. Benscheidt Sr. 1947, p. 306.

18   E.g., Neufert 1936, p. 188. He published only a site plan bearing the caption, "Plan for a factory complex on railroad with possibility for expansion toward the country road," without mentioning either the name of the company or the architect. There is no commentary whatsoever on the architecture. See also E. Neufert, in: *Wasmuths Lexikon der Baukunst*, Vol. 5 (Berlin 1937), under "Fabriken," [factories] on p. 178.

19   K. Benscheidt Jr. 1927, p. 295.

20   C. Benscheidt Sr. 1947, p. 322. Facsimile of Gropius's application letter in Weber 1961, p. 29.

21   *Cf.* the description of how the commission was secured by Ernst Neufert, building manager for Gropius's office in Alfeld from 1923–1924, in Wilhelm 1983, p. 134, fn. 283. Neufert's knowledge cannot be based on firsthand experience but rather only gathered from accounts by Gropius or Benscheidt.

22   C. Benscheidt Sr. to W. Gropius, letter from January 12, 1911. Copy H. Weber, Hanover. See Weber 1961, p. 30.

23   C. Benscheidt Sr. to W. Gropius, letter dated January 12, 1911. Copy H. Weber, Hanover.

24   W. Gropius to C. Benscheidt Sr., letter dated January 13, 1911. Copy H. Weber, Hanover.

25   Draft for letter by W. Gropius to A. Mahler, undated (circa September 1910), BHA Pos. 8/1.3.

26   E.g. Dieling 1936, p. 48, on the occasion of the twenty-fifth anniversary of the Fagus factory. Members of the Benscheidt family still today emphasize Meyer's importance.

27   This was common knowledge at the time. In reference to the Fagus factory, Bruno Taut attributes the stunningly "clean lines" of the building to Meyer. See B. Taut: "Adolf Meyer." In: *Das Neue Berlin* I. 1929, H.9, p. 183. On the question of the collaboration between Gropius and Meyer and their respective contributions, see Jaeggi 1994 and 1995.

28   Lost after Meyer's death in 1929. A list in the estate (BHA) provides an overview of the planning material, which he had stored at one point.

29   C. Benscheidt Sr. 1947, p. 322. W. Gropius to C. Benscheidt Sr., letter dated February 6, 1911 (contract conditions). Copy H. Weber, Hanover.

30   W. Gropius to C. Benscheidt Sr., no date, probably

circa February 13, 1911 (stamp of receipt: February 14, 1911). Copy H. Weber, Hanover. *Cf.* Weber 1961, p. 43.

31 Ibid.

32 C. Benscheidt Sr., to W. Gropius, letter dated March 20, 1911. Copy H. Weber, Hanover. See Weber 1961, p. 30.

33 Ibid.

34 W. Gropius to H. Weber, letter dated May 10, 1959. BHA, Gropius-Weber correspondence.

35 The only surviving document is a photograph of plan. Photo-Archives Marburg, No. 1072499. Gropius probably gave this photo to the Stoedtner archives. It may be identical with the "recently completed elevation of my factory complex in Alfeld," which he mailed to Osthaus at the beginning of September 1911. *Cf.* W. Gropius to K. E. Osthaus, letter dated Sept. 7, 1911. KEOA, Kü 319/28.

36 W. Gropius to C. Benscheidt Sr., letter dated April 8, 1911. Copy H. Weber, Hanover.

37 Fagus archives, reg. No. 448. This drawing is dated in Meyer's handwriting "May 1911" and carries on the back side a received by Fagus factory stamp from May 21, 1911.

38 C. Benscheidt Sr. to F. Cox, letter dated April 26, 1911. Fagus archives, file 295.

39 C. Benscheidt Sr. 1947, p. 322.

40 C. Benscheidt Sr. to W. Gropius, letter dated May 13, 1911. BHA, GN 201.

41 C. Benscheidt Sr. 1947, p. 322.

42 C. Benscheidt Sr. to F. Cox, letter dated August 9, 1911. Fagus archives, file 295.

43 C. Benscheidt Sr. to W. Gropius, letter dated June 16, 1911. Copy H. Weber, Hanover.

44 C. Benscheidt Sr. to W. Gropius, letter dated September 1, 1911. Copy H. Weber, Hanover.

45 W. Gropius to C. Benscheidt Sr., letter dated September 2, 1911. Partial copy H. Weber, Hanover. There is no surviving copy of the girder plan.

46 K. Benscheidt Jr. explained the Gropius knot with the comment that the original construction was modified because one of the delivered girders was too short. *Cf.* H. Weber to W. Gropius, letter dated April 13, 1960. BHA, Gropius-Weber correspondence. This is contradicted by the repeated use of the solution, which, incidentally, is already indictated in the plan on "Sheet 1" from May 1911.

47 Gropius 1965, p. 134. *Cf.* Götz contribution in this volume.

48 *Cf.* Götz contribution in this volume.

49 Beutinger 1913, p. 13, maintains that "all window-panes are uniformly identical in size." However, this statement does not live up to closer inspection.

50 Nolan 1994, p. 19, notes this contradictory behavior during the 1920s. It may also be applicable to the pre–World War I era.

51 Gropius 1911 (Monumentale Kunst und Industriebau); see Probst/Schädlich 1988, p. 45.

52 C. Benscheidt Sr. to F. Cox, letter dated January 6, 1913. Fagus archives, file 295.

53 C. Benscheidt Sr. to F. Cox, letter dated December 18, 1911. Fagus archives, file 295.

54 Ibid.

55 Banham 1986, p. 194.

56 For more detailed information, refer to J. Götz's chapter. See also Weber's drawing from 1961, p. 63.

57 W. Gropius to H. Weber, letter dated June 12, 1959. BHA, Gropius correspondence. See also Gropius 1965, p. 136.

58 Handwritten note by A. Meyer on drawing sheet 156 from July 24, 1914. Fagus archives, registration No. 131.

59 Drawing sheet 155 from July 24, 1914, modified on February 12, 1915. Fagus archives, registration No. 139.

60 *Cf.* the description of the building permission application from November 18, 1915. Alfeld Building Authorities, file on Hanoversche Strasse 231, Vol. IV, 1915–1926. Excerpts published in: Wilhelm 1983, p. 47.

61 Ibid.

62 W. Gropius to M. Gropius, letter dated June 30, 1916. BHA, Gropius private correspondence, display case 8.

1 Behne 1913–1914, p. 53, and Behne 1914, p. 215.

2 *Cf.* W. Hildebrandt, P. Lemburg, and J. Wewel: *Historische Bauwerke der Berliner Industrie. Beiträge zur Denkmalpflege in Berlin*, No. 1 (Berlin 1988), p. 38*ff.* The authors maintain, and rightly so, that even in the nineteenth century, renowned architects had created sophisticated designs for factory buildings.

3 Grimshaw 1913, p. 21. The works library at Fagus contained a copy of this book.

4 *Cf.* Nerdinger 1997. The *Bund Deutscher Architekten* (Association of German Architects) identified itself with this term in *Neudeutsche Bauzeitung*, a magazine founded by the association in 1905. Behrens created the title page and the layout for the magazine.

5 Hoeber 1913, p. 115.

6 W. Gropius to G. Hoeltje, letter of June 5, 1958. BHA, Gropius-Hoeltje correspondence. *Cf.* Weber 1961, p. 23.

7 Posener 1979, pp. 564–570, examines this relationship in a detailed comparison of the Turbine factory and the main building of the Fagus factory.

8 Behne 1913, p. 173.

9 W. Gropius: Lecture "Monumentale Kunst und Industriebau" (Monumental Art and Industrial Building) given at the Folkwang museum in Hagen on April 10, 1911. Typescript with pasted photographs, BHA. *Cf.* Probst/ Schädlich 1988, pp. 28–51, here p. 29.

10 Behrens 1910. *Cf.* Buddensieg/Rogge, p. D 277.

Ausst.kat. (Exhib. cat.) Exhibition catalog

BHA (BHA) Bauhaus Archiv Berlin

BRM (BRM) Busch-Reisinger Museum, Harvard University, Cambridge, MA

Fagus-Archiv (Fagus archives) Fagus archives, Ernst and Gerd Greten. On permanent loan at the Bauhaus Archiv Berlin

HStA Weimar (HStA) Central Archives of the State of Thuringia, Weimar

Inv. Nr. (Inventory No.) inventory number

JMC (JMC) Johannes-Molzahn-Centrum, Kassel

KEOA (KEOA) Karl Ernst Osthaus Archives, Hagen

Kopie H. Weber (Copy H. Weber) Photocopies or typewriter copies of correspondence between C. Benscheidt Sr. and W. Gropius, private collection of Prof. Dr. H. Weber, Hanover. Originals formerly stored in the Fagus archives.

Kat. Nr. (Cat. No.) catalog number

Obj. Nr. (Obj. No.) object number

Reg. Nr. (Reg. No.) registration number

WLM (WLM) Wilhelm Lehmbruck Museum, Duisburg

Gropius 1911 (Monumentale Kunst und Industriebau); *cf.* Probst/Schädlich 1988, pp. 48*ff.*

11 *Cf.* note 9. The lecture was first entitled "Die künstlerische Entwicklung im Industriebau. Praktische Vorschläge" (Artistic Development in Industrial Building. Practical Suggestions), then "Kunst und Industriebau" (Art and Industrial Building), before the final title was found. *Cf.* correspondence between Gropius and Osthaus. KEOA, Kü 318/13–18.

12 *Cf.* Hesse-Frielinghaus 1971; Exhibition catalog 1993–1994; Exhibition catalog 1997–1998.

13 Isaacs 1983, p. 106. C. Benscheidt Sr. to W. Gropius, letter dated June 16, 1911. Copy H. Weber, Hanover. Benscheidt contributed 20 marks to the building fund in addition to the 10-mark annual subscription fee.

14 *Cf.* Jaeggi 1994, p. 70 with notes 95 and 98.

15 How strongly Gropius identified with this philosophy, even claiming it as his own, is evident in the draft of a letter to A. Mahler dated April 11, 1911: "Yesterday I presented my lecture on monumental art and industrial building in the beautiful lecture hall of Osthaus's Folkwangmuseum in Hagen in front of an audience that included some very important people. My revolutionary ideas, which delivered some heavy blows to the art materialists, at least made some of these people—the most influential in the crowd—pause and reflect, and this satisfies me deeply." BHA, Gropius, private correspondence, Pos. 2/1, 3.

16 Behne 1913, p. 171; the following quote, p. 172.

17 Behne 1913–1914, p. 61.

18 Even in 1924, W. Gropius's wife Ise Gropius complained that the Fagus factory was "located in such a small town and was therefore so little known." Diary of Ise Gropius, entry for October/November 1924, BHA.

19 Manuscript, 6 sheets. BHA, Gropius estate, box: manuscripts up to 1919. The following quotes are taken from the same source. Gropius mentions "my piece on artistic urge" in several of the drafted letters to A. Mahler in connection with the spa holiday in Tobelbad in June/July of 1910, during which stay he had first met her.

20 Riegl 1901. Gropius was probably aware of Riegl's writings through Behrens, who had used them as a reference on which to base his own theories: e.g., Behrens 1909; *cf.* Buddensieg/Rogge, p. D 280.

21 Gropius 1911 (Monumentale Kunst und Industriebau); *cf.* Probst/Schädlich 1988, p. 28.

22 Gropius 1910. The following quote is taken from the same source.

23 Hoeber 1913, p. 114. *Cf.* Riegl 1927, p. 33*ff.*

24 Gropius 1910. On how the speed in modern transportation influenced architecture, see: Behrens 1909; *cf.* Buddensieg/Rogge, p. D 284.

25 Draft of letter by W. Gropius to A. Mahler, undated, circa 1910. BHA, Gropius private correspondence, Pos. 7/3.

26 Draft of letter by W. Gropius to A. Mahler, January 23, 1911. BHA, W. Gropius private correspondence, Pos. 6/11.

27 *Cf.* Jaeggi 1994, p. 77 and Obj. No. 7, p. 237*ff.*

28 Weber 1961, pp. 66 and 75. In executing the first cor-

ner without piers (east) Gropius and Meyer were forced through Werner's placement of piers (at 5-meter intervals) to glaze the remaining 2.65 meters with different-sized panes. Only once these wider panes had also been installed on the west corner did this solution appear to be deliberate.

29 Weber 1961, p. 65. We now know that several of the floor-height iron sashes were to be replaced in the intervening years, whole corner sections have been restored, and that the iron frames, which had not stood up to fluctuations in temperature, warped up to 6 centimeters in some instances (see section by J. Götz). Hence, Weber's precision must be seen as less than absolute. However, this does not alter the fundamental results.

30 Gropius 1956, p. 35. In direct reference to the different sizes of the window panes in the main building of the Fagus factory construction noted by Weber, Rudolf Hillebrecht reminded Gropius in a letter dated January 19, 1961, of their joint visit to the Pergamonmuseum in 1934. During that visit, Gropius had given Hillebrecht a lesson on the treatment of proportion and its effect in antiquity using the models of Priene and Miletus as examples. BHA, Gropius-Hillebrecht correspondence.

31 Ludwig Max Goldberger: *Das Land der unbegrenzten Möglichkeiten.* Berlin 1903.

32 Holitscher 1912, p. 426.

33 Holitscher 1912, p. 140*ff.* with photographs of silos in the Canadian cities Fort William and Port Arthur. The Fort William image corresponds to Gropius 1913, fig. after p. 22. The precursors to these silos, which did not yet have the typical cylindrical shape, had already become an attraction on trips to America. *Cf.* v. Hesse-Wartegg 1908, fig. p. 239 (Chicago) and p. 315 (Duluth). On the history of the American silo, see also Banham 1986, chapter 2, "The Grain Elevator," p. 109*ff.*

34 Gropius 1913. Printed (without photo illustrations) in: Probst/Schädlich 1988, pp. 55–57. On how American silos were received in reaction to this publication, see also Cohen 1995, pp. 63–68.

35 Exhibition catalog 1993–1994, p. 17.

36 "I'll gladly get these architectural things for you—the only difficulty is a lack of English terminology—but I'll try!" A. Mahler to W. Gropius, letter from November 8, 1910. See also letters from November 23 and 30, 1910. BHA, Gropius private correspondence. Gropius's letters to Alma Mahler have been lost.

37 KEOA, 318/10.

38 For example: "Silo und Elevator der Baltimore & Ohio Eisenbahn-Gesellschaft in Baltimore" (Probst/Schädlich 1988, p. 49, fig. 64), in: *Beton und Eisen* 8. 1909, No. 10 (July 22), p. 245. "Korn-Silo in Buenos Aires" (Probst/Schädlich 1988, p. 50, fig. 69), in: *Beton und Eisen* 9. 1910, No. 3 (February 20), p. 77. For information on the photo credits in this magazine, see: W. Nerdinger: "Fotografien amerikanischer Getreidespeicher. Ikonen der modernen Architektur." In: G. Engel: *Buffalo Grain Elevators* (Munich 1997), pp. 5–9, here p. 6.

39 W. Gropius to K. E. Osthaus, letter dated August 8, 1911. KEOA, Kü 319/16.

40 "I'm happy to fulfil your wish [stated on the] thir-
teenth of this month by sending you the postcards
which I have." C. Benscheidt Sr. to W. Gropius, letter
dated March 20, 1911. Copy H. Weber, Hanover.
This must be the source of Banham's "once-current
legend," 1986, p. 195, according to which Benscheidt
Sr. had given Gropius a parcel with photographs from
America. There are no photographs of American
buildings in the Fagus archives, even of the United
Shoe Machinery Corporation in Beverly,
Massachusetts, the company which was the financial
backer of the Fagus GmbH.

41 K. Benscheidt Jr. to O. Lüken, letter dated August 28,
1912. Fagus archives, file 29.

42 Gropius 1913, p. 21; cf. Probst/Schädlich 1988,
p. 57.

43 Riegl 1927, p. 38.

44 Gropius, 1913, p. 21 cf. Probst/Schädlich 1988, p. 57.

45 See also: W. Pehnt: "Altes Ägypten und neues Bauen.
Der Einfluß der Pharaonenkunst auf die Moderne."
In: W. Pehnt Die Erfindung der Geschichte (Munich
1989), pp. 68–86.

46 Gropius 1911 (Monumentale Kunst und
Industriebau); cf. Probst/Schädlich1988, p. 50.

47 Gropius 1911 (Monumentale Kunst und
Industriebau); cf. Probst/Schädlich 1988, p. 30.

48 Gropius 1913, p. 22; cf. Probst/Schädlich 1988, p. 57.

49 Behne 1913, p. 172.

50 Behne 1913–1914, pp. 59–62.

51 Behne 1922, p. 638, and Behne 1926 (manuscript
from 1923), p. 27. Friedrich Ostendorf (1871–1915)
sought to create an artistic effect with a closed and
axial building structure based on late-eighteenth-
century neoclassicism: severe order and ultimate
simplicity.

52 Draft of letter from W. Gropius to A. Mahler, undated, BHA, Gropius private correspondence, Pos. 7/1.

53 A. Paquet to K. E. Osthaus, letter dated March 8,
1911. KEOA, DWB 75/20-21.

54 Journals for the concrete industry commonly took this
to be the advantage of concrete versus iron; e.g. Beton
und Eisen, prior to World War I.

55 Gropius 1911 (Monumentale Kunst und
Industriebau); cf. Probst/Schädlich 1988, p. 29.

56 Behrens 1910; cf. Buddensieg/Rogge, p. D 277.

57 Behrens 1909; cf. Buddensieg/Rogge, p. D 283.
Hoeber 1913, p. 113.

58 Gropius 1911 (Monumentale Kunst und
Industriebau); cf. Probst/Schädlich 1988, p. 33.

59 According to Neufert, Gropius still used the
bridge example in 1955 when the Ulm School of
Design was inaugurated. Cf. Jaeggi 1994, p. 118
and fn. 92.

60 Gropius 1911 (Monumentale Kunst und
Industriebau); cf. Probst/Schädlich 1988, p. 29ff.

61 Ironically, Poelzig disagreed with Behrens and
Gropius; he felt that "the aesthetic of iron construction lies completely . . . in the expression of the net-
like framework and in the ever smaller scale of the
individual components of the construction." He too
used an iron bridge as an example, albeit to illustrate
"a perfect impression . . . in the dissolution of the
individual building components, in making the mater-

ial invisible . . overcoming enormous distances with
an almost incorporeal grace." Poelzig 1911, p. 103ff.

62 Hoeber 1913, p. 113, uses this term, derived from
Riegl, to describe the Turbine hall.

63 Based loosely on Gropius 1956, p. 34 (1982 edition, p.
43). The observations put forth in that text were with
regard to the Indian temple. They are proof of the
lasting influence of Riegl's theory on Gropius, even
into his mature work.

64 Riegl 1927, p. 33.

65 Gropius 1911 (Monumentale Kunst und
Industriebau); cf. Probst/Schädlich 1988, p. 29.

66 Diary of Ise Gropius, entry on February 9, 1926.
BHA. Characteristically, as in 1911, Gropius seeks to
anchor his ideas in history—that is, in the religious
building of the "Egyptians, Arabs, and the Gothic
style." However, with neither religious thought nor a
common view of life [according to Gropius] to create
a cultural basis for society in 1926, "the new idea of
building and new spatial concepts are now only manifest in abstract creations, which do, however, give an
idea of what the future laws of building will be."

67 Gropius 1926, p. 160. This article illustrates the
Bauhaus building, as well as the Werkbund model factory and the Fagus factory. Although not explicitly
stated, the figure of the Fagus factory serves as proof
of the new approach to spatial perception and gives
the impression that the building was constructed with
the new materials, steel and concrete.

68 C. Benscheidt Sr.: Die Gründung des Fagus-Werks
(The Founding of the Fagus Factory). Manuscript
from 1938, p. 12. Fagus archives.

69 Gropius 1911 (Monumentale Kunst und
Industriebau); cf. Probst/Schädlich 1988, p. 31.

70 Behne 1922, p. 639: "Already the first Fagus building
had given room to the use of glass such as it had hitherto only been known in department-store buildings."
Hegemann 1929, p. 25: "The magnificent Leipziger
Street front of the Wertheim building [architect A.
Messel, 1985] was later outshone by the glass curtains
in the Tietz warehouse [architect B. Sehring,
1899/1900] and the provincial latecomer of the
Bauhaus at Dessau."

71 C. Benscheidt Sr. to J. H. Connor, letter dated
December 29, 1910, sheet 7. Fagus archives,
file 294.

72 Cf. G. P. Carver: "Reinforced Concrete Building
Work for the United Shoe Machinery Co., Beverly,
Mass." In: Engineering News 53. 1905, issue No. 21
(May 25), pp. 537–543. Banham 1986, chapter I
"The Daylight Factory," p. 23ff., on USMC, see pp.
68–71.

73 Scheffler 1911, p. 234. In an undated letter, Gropius
recommended this essay, from which he adapted for-
mulations for his texts, to C. Benscheidt Sr. (probably
from February 13, 1911; stamped "received" at Fagus
factory on February 14, 1911). Copy H. Weber,
Hanover.

74 The Steiff factory was mentioned for the first time by
M. Cetto: "eine fabrik von 1903." In: die neue stadt
1932, No. 4, p. 88. cf. Reiff 1992.

75 Gropius 1911 (Monumentale Kunst und
Industriebau); cf. Probst/Schädlich 1988, p. 29.

1 C. Benscheidt Sr. to F. Cox, letter dated Nov. 5, 1920. Fagus archives, file 297.

2 Furthermore, shoe fashion played an important role. From 1925 onward, it changed less in form than in design and in color. *Cf.* the eighteen-page report on the development of the German shoe-last industry, written by C. Benscheidt Sr. on Nov. 2, 1928, for J.F. Connor. Fagus archives, file 22. On the effect of rationalization circa 1925–1926, see Nolan 1994, p. 132, fn. 5.

3 Westheim 1925.

4 C. Benscheidt Sr. to J.H. Connor, letter dated July 10, 1910. Fagus archives, file 294.

5 This is how he measured the work speed—that is, the production performance within a specific period of time. In addition, he considered "whether one could not increase the performance of a worker if one were to assign him to a task where he has to stand for half of the day and another task where he has to sit for the other half." The notebooks are stored in the Fagus archives. On Taylor, see also Giedion 1982, p. 122*ff*.

6 In one of the American factory notebooks, Benscheidt Jr. was already encouraging the use of quality control workers.

7 An entry in Benscheidt's address book points to the possibility of such a meeting. He probably met Ford during his second stay in the United States in 1928. The address book is stored in the Fagus archives.

8 K. Benscheidt Jr. 1927, p. 290; the following quote is taken from p. 303.

9 According to Nolan 1994, pp. 89 and 97, the well-trained and versatile quality worker is a German phenomenon, as is the aptitude test by means of psychological examinations.

10 Karl Benscheidt—that is, the junior manager, is named in the list of the art manifesto issued by the Workers' Council. The relevant literature—exhibition catalog *Arbeitsrat für Kunst 1918–1921*, Akademie der Künste Berlin (1980), p. 128, and E. Steneberg: *Arbeitsrat für Kunst, Berlin 1918–1921* (Düsseldorf 1987), p. 89—contains the erroneous assumption that the name referred to the senior manager.

11 Diary of Ise Gropius, entry from September 3, 1924. BHA. *Cf.* Jaeggi 1994, pp. 130*f*.

12 *Cf.* "Aufstellung der bisher gezeichneten G.m.b.H.-Anteile" from December 8, 1924, BHA, archives Walter Gropius, file 74. See also letters by K. Benscheidt Jr. to W. Gropius in January and February 1925. Municipal Archives, Dessau, SB/17 (Kreis der Freunde des Bauhauses, 1925–1933).

13 Untitled manuscript dated November 21, 1922. Fagus archives, file 135. The following quote is from the same source.

14 Manuscript "Der Direktor des Staatl. Bauhauses spricht in Alfeld," dated January 10, 1923, two sheets, Fagus archives, file 135.

15 A. Meyer to H. Müller, letter dated July 3, 1924. HStA Weimar, Bauhaus archives, file 56, sheet 55f.

16 Weber reports in 1961, p. 50, that Gropius was involved in designing the ironing tool. After Gropius, Benscheidt Jr. also commissioned Molzahn to create designs for the socket. There is no documentation as to who created the design we know today. *Cf.* letter by J. Molzahn to K. Benscheidt. Jr. dated April 15, 1922. JMC. According to Reuter, 1925, p. 245, "the artist/architect spoke a decisive word with regard to the construction of the machines."

17 *Cf.* exhibition catalog *Die zwanziger Jahre in Hanover*, Kunstverein Hanover, 1962, p. 108. According to E. Steneberg: *Arbeitsrat für Kunst, Berlin 1918–1921* (Düsseldorf 1987), p. 104, Benscheidt Jr. also participated in the foundation of the Kestner society in 1916.

18 Benscheidt Jr. lists K. Dreier in his address book. Fagus archives.

19 Based on the expense accounts (receipt book) of the junior manager, one can reconstruct visits by artist friends, as they were usually invited to lunch or dinner. His address book is also a valuable source of information.

20 In a letter to J. Molzahn dated July 11, 1924, he criticized the model issue of *G*, which had been mailed to him. WLM.

21 Weinert 1927, p. 78.

22 Weinert 1927. The Fagus archives contains sections of Weinert's scientific estate, among them vintage prints (approximately eighty different motifs) and the corresponding glass negative plates by Renger-Patzsch.

23 *Cf.* Renger-Patzsch's comments in his correspondence with A. Weinert from 1928, Fagus archives, file 205.

24 Heckert (1997, p. 20, fn. 45) was the first to draw attention to the photographs taken for Weinert . In Renger-Patzsch's own view of himself as an artist, he probably thought of these photographs, as well as of the Angulus Varus series, as merely commercial work undertaken to pay the bills.

25 Angulus Varus Society (Eds.): *Der Angulus Varus Schuh*. No year, circa 1928, 18 fig. The Fagus archives contain only a few vintage prints, but nineteen negative plates.

26 As another series indicates, during the film two children join in the scene and try on Angulus Varus shoes. Fifteen negative plates in the Fagus archives.

27 *Cf.* Jaeggi 1994, Obj. No. 173, pp. 411–414; Obj. No. 179b, pp. 419*f*.

28 *Cf.* Gropius in 1910: "Each level surface has its specific light intensity; white reflects, black absorbs. . . . The ornamentation in antiquity is based on this fact. Preference is given to the light contrast shape versus the dark background shape. The perfect solution lies in harmoniously balancing these two contrasting elements (force and counterforce)."

29 *Cf.* the commemorative plaque at the war memorial in Ollendorf near Weimar, a Bauhaus design, for which no individual artist has been indicated. The unveiling

took place on April 30, 1922.

30 P. Fumanek. Color study report for the staircase at the Fagus factory. Hanover 1989–1990 (unpublished).

31 We cannot be more specific in the date than 1922, as no date was indicated for the completion. On the Gropius handle, see also Jaeggi 1994, Obj. No. 175, pp. 415f.

32 This discrepancy was also noted by K. Benscheidt Jr. in a letter to H. M. Wingler dated July 3, 1970. BHA. In the letter, the junior manager describes the handle as "the handcrafted handle on our main entrance doors."

33 K.-J. Sembach: *Möbel, die Geschichte machen* (Hamburg 1988), p. 33. See Jaeggi 1994, Obj. No. 165d, pp. 402f, unaware of the drawings at the time, stylistically attributed to the time around 1923–1924, and erroneously placed in the third floor.

34 *Staatliches Bauhaus Weimar 1919–1923.* (Munich and Weimar 1923), fig. 34ff.

35 *Cf.* questionnaire on his time at the Bauhaus completed by E. Brendel in 1965. BHA.

36 This hypothesis was last once again proposed by Wetzel 1995, pp. 8–11; on the variations of the door handle design at the Fagus factory, see also pp. 23 and 25, fig. 1–2 and 13–15 of the same source.

37 Schadendorf 1958, p. 8.

38 *Cf.* Jaeggi 1994, Obj. No. 52, pp. 313–315.

39 Reuter 1925, p. 243.

40 Receipt book of Benscheidt Jr., November 1919 until April 1925, Fagus archives.

41 *Cf.* the monthly reports for the mural painting workshop from March and April 1924, HStA Weimar, Bauhaus documents, file 177, sheet 20f.

42 In a letter to H.M. Wingler dated July 3, 1970 (BHA), K. Benscheidt Jr. reports that the new wing from 1913–1914 was "now fully equipped with Bauhaus door handles, in contrast to the northeast section, built in 1911." That is, in 1970 there were no Gropius handles in the original office floor (or only a few, which would have been installed on the interior doors during the renovation works in 1924).

43 Reuter 1925, p. 245.

44 H. Scheper to L. Scheper, letter dated February 5, 1923. Private collection.

45 Folder "Erbschein Carl Benscheidt Sr." Private collection.

46 *Cf.* Wilhelm 1983, pp. 203f, figs. 90–92.

47 Based on exactly datable photographs, the wall, a mere 11 centimeters thick and stretched between two masoned pillars, was torn down after 1950.

48 In a letter to H. Weber dated April 18, 1960, W. Gropius wrote: "The Schmiede [*sic*; referring to the tool-and-die shop] I never liked very much; the building is too conventional and Mr. Benscheidt, at that time, pushed this building very much so that there was no time for the necessary research to renew that conception." BHA, correspondence Gropius-Weber.

49 C. Benscheidt Sr. to Mr. Stolze, letter dated June 13, 1927, Fagus archives, file 228.

50 Contract draft dated June 3, 1930, Fagus archives, file 272.

51 W. Gropius to C. Benscheidt Sr., letter dated April 26, 1936. BHA, correspondence Gropius-Benscheidt, 8/42.

52 W. Gropius to C. Benscheidt Sr., letter dated December 15, 1936, BHA, correspondence Gropius-Benscheidt, 8/39. *Cf.* the positive comment by Gropius on Scharoun in a letter to M. Wagner from December 27, 1936, printed in: P. Hahn (Ed.): *bauhaus berlin* (Weingarten 1985), pp. 228f.

1 C. Benscheidt Sr. 1947, p. 326.

2 Ibid.

3 Beutinger 1913; Reuter 1925, Hoffmann 1930.

4 C. Benscheidt Sr. 1947, p. 325

5 The 1927 newspaper and magazine catalog of Rudolf Mosse Expedition, p. 270, lists thirty trade magazines for the shoe industry in Germany alone.

6 C. Benscheidt Sr. to W. Gropius, letter dated October 26, 1911. Copy of excerpts, H. Weber, Hanover. *Cf.* C. Benscheidt Sr. to F. Cox, letter dated December 18, 1911. Fagus archives, file 295.

7 Whether Hertwig's design was published in the 1911 Christmas issue of *Schuh und Leder* is still unclear; copies of the issues are unavailable at the Fagus archives and in German libraries.

8 This is how Fritz Adolphy, another graduate of the School of Arts and Crafts in Düsseldorf and short-term employee at Behrens, was instructed by Gropius to label the photo displays in the exhibition *Vorbildliche Industriebauten*. A notebook entry by Benscheidt Jr. alludes to the fact that Adolphy may also have worked at Fagus; however, this has not been proved.

9 K. Benscheidt Jr. to J. Molzahn, letter dated April 6, 1922. WLM.

10 Werkbund members had already distanced themselves from this idea for some time. *Cf.* letterhead collection in: exhibition catalog Krefeld 1997–1998, pp. 226f.

11 The correspondence has been preserved both in the WLM and in the JMC; both institutions have provided each other with photocopies to complete the missing pieces of correspondence in each location.

12 Molzahn 1926.

13 J. Molzahn to K. Benscheidt Jr., letter dated February 26, 1922. JMC.

14 J. Molzahn to I. Molzahn, letter dated March 31, 1922. National Library Berlin, manuscript department, estate Ilse Molzahn, 161, box 43.

15 J. Molzahn to K. Benscheidt Jr., letter dated March 14, 1922. JMC.

16 J. Molzahn to K. Benscheidt Jr., letter dated January 26, 1923. WLM.

17 K. Benscheidt Jr. to J. Molzahn, letter dated July 19, 1923. WLM. K. Benscheidt Jr.'s letter to W. Gropius dated July 5, 1923, should be taken in the same con-

text; in this letter, he indicates that he "would like to speak with you about our advertising." HStA Weimar, Bauhaus material, file 32, sheet 54. Quote from exhibition catalog 1995–1996, cat. No. 273, p. 306, which has been erroneously interpreted as indicating that Fagus commissioned the Bauhaus to create advertising material for print.

18 K. Benscheidt Jr. to J. Molzahn, letter dated May 16, 1922. WLM.

19 K. Benscheidt Jr. to J. Molzahn, letter dated October 10, 1923. WLM.

20 K. Benscheidt Jr. to J. Molzahn, letter dated February 1, 1924. WLM.

21 BHA (donation from H. Bayer), marked 1925 on the back, bottom right in pencil. The business card was not yet designed in the DIN format, which was used at the Bauhaus only after August 1925.

22 Cf. exhibition catalog 1995–1996, cat. No. 272, p. 306.

23 A different version reproduced in: Offset 1926, No. 7, plate 23, where it is dated 1925.

24 Alternating ads were to introduce a different product on each title page of the trade magazine Schuhfabrikanten-Zeitung. The first ad about shoe lasts was created by Molzahn in January 1925. Cf. W. Hanstein to J. Molzahn, letter dated December 3, 1924. WLM.

25 Tschichold 1928, p. 160.

26 BHA, inventory No. 7294 (donation by H. Bayer). Reproduced and dated 1925 in: Offset 1926, issue 7, pp. 380ff., plate 23.

27 Cf. diary of Ise Gropius, entry dated September 18, 1925: "the Bauhaus has introduced lowercase type for typographical reasons and to save time. Dessau is in an uproar, but it will probably be pushed through." BHA.

28 BHA, inventory No. 8702 and 8716 (donated by H. Bayer).

29 BHA, inventory No. 8709/I (donated by H. Bayer), marked 1926 in pencil on front side, bottom right.

30 The photograph dated 1928 as well as the new telephone number for the Fagus factory after June 1928 are helpful in establishing a date.

31 On June 5, 1926, Ise Gropius wrote in her diary about "lots of aggravation at the Bauhaus. Benscheidt has returned printed matter as unusable for Fagus." BHA.

32 Fagus archives, advertising folder and file 260. Even though there is no concrete proof that Benscheidt Jr. wrote the copy for the sales folders designed by Bayer, these documents contradict Brüning's assumption from 1988, p. 174, that the text as well as the concept for the Fagus sales folders had been created in the Bauhaus workshop.

33 W. Hanstein to J. Molzahn, letter dated December 3, 1924. WLM. After August 1924, K. Benscheidt Jr. introduced so-called stock numbers, consisting of numbers and capital letters, for all print items. In the case of the sales folders, the numbering began with Molzahn's "Stützmesser" folder as K1 and was continued for the work designed by Bayer. K is the initial for Katalog; S stands for Stegen, the print shop in Alfeld.

34 Ise Gropius. Diary, entry dated January 30, 1925. BHA. Schwitters, who had held a lecture in Dessau on the previous evening, tells her the story. See also K. Benscheidt Jr.'s receipt book, November 1919 to April 1925. Fagus archives.

35 Donation from van Moorsel, inventory No. AB 5003. Cf. E. v. Straaten: Theo van Doesburg 1883–1931 (The Hague 1983), p. 25.

36 K. Benscheidt Jr. to T. v. Doesburg, letter dated January 21, 1929. Rijksbureau voor kunsthistorische Documentatie The Hague. Theo van Doesburg archives, inventory No. 234. I would like to thank Ute Brüning, Berlin, for making this letter available.

1 According to Heckert 1997, p. 6, E. Neufert (who became director of architecture at the State School of Architecture in Weimar in 1926) was probably introduced to Renger-Patzsch's work through K. Benscheidt Jr. This led to the school offering Renger-Patzsch a teaching position at the end of 1927.

2 Beutinger, 1913.

3 In contrast to the newly erected Behrens shoe last factory, featured in Schuhmarkt; Cf.: Anon. 1899.

4 Gropius 1911–1912 and 1912.

5 Because C. Benscheidt Sr. ordered 1500 special-edition prints of this report for advertising purposes, one can assume that the editor, who was also the author, may have taken his clients wishes into consideration.

6 Cf. Jaeggi, 1994, obj. No. 136, pp. 376–380.

7 E. Lill: Mein Leben, mein Streben & Ziel. Manuscript, 1954. Private collection.

8 Edmund Lill worked at his brother's headquarters in Mannheim during the same period as Hugo Schmölz, the photographer of architecture who later worked in Cologne. Cf. K.-H. Schmölz and R. Sachsse (eds.): Hugo Schmölz. Fotografierte Architektur 1924–1937 (Munich 1982).

9 Cf. Exhibition catalog 1990, p. 151.

10 Christian Wolsdorff, BHA, attended to this painstaking task. My observations are based on his findings.

11 BHA and BRM. The collection of the former German Museum for Art in Trade and Production at Hagen (now part of the Kaiser Wilhelm Museum in Krefeld) as well as the Stoedtner Photo Archives (now assimilated into the Marburg Image Archives) contains photographs of Fagus by Lill. The quality suggests that these are not prints from the plate, but contemporary reproductions. Cf. Exhibition catalog Krefeld 1993–1994, cat. 235–239, pp. 194. and 213.

12 It is difficult to prove that Lill created these photographs. Only a few architecture photos have survived as vintage prints, some in the estates of Gropius and Meyer. The references to the original negatives

are not marked on the back side of the prints. On the other hand, the photographic paper and a few handwritten comments speak for Lill.

13 *Cf.* K. Benscheidt Jr. to J. Molzahn, letter dated June 23, 1922. WLM.

14 Based on how often requests are received at the Bauhaus archives for the Fagus photographs, these images are among the most popular of this era.

15 This is supported by Renger-Patzsch's presence in Alfeld on April 26 and 27, 1928. Benscheidt Jr.'s receipt book shows that he entertained the photographer. All prints are stamped on the back by Renger-Patzsch. Approximately half of the photographs date from the Bad Harzburg period. Among the architecture photographs, there are some with the Essen stamp; the thin photographic paper may indicate that they were a second set. The 1928 series should not be confused with the second series from 1952, where Renger-Patzsch re-created some of his earlier shots. The later series is invariably stamped "Wamel Dorf" (Wamel village).

16 This is also supported by sketches for ads in Benscheidt Jr.'s advertising folder for publication in Switzerland. Still, there is no proof that any Renger-Patzsch photographs were actually used for this purpose.

17 Numbers 2, 5, 6, 11, 20, 21, 28, 35, 40, 50, 52, and 53 are missing.

18 Dieling 1936, p. 57. The back is marked "Buchenwald/Fagus" and carries a stamp from Renger-Patzsch's Bad Harzburg period.

19 In: *Hauff-Leonar Mitteilungen* 1929, No. 2 (probably March), p. 23. The telephone poles in the background are a sure hint that the locale was the lumber yard of the Fagus factory. This may be photograph number 28 from the series. I'd like to thank Christian Wolsdorff for the tip.

20 There are American examples in the Fagus archives: O.A. Miller Treeing Machine Co. (ed.): *Illustrated Catalogue of Parts for Miller No. 2 Electric Ironing Equipment* (Brockton, Mass. undated, circa 1913) and *No. 3 Electric Equipment* (Brockton, Mass., undated).

21 "The first photograph should be of the tree in the woods (Fagus = beech), the pendulum saw, the large belt saw, the roughing lathe, drying kilns, etc." Typescript from April 15, 1919, titled "client advertising." Fagus archives, file 133.

22 Renger photographs sent to the editorial department: numbers 8, 16, 22, 34, 51, and 54. *Cf.* K. Benscheidt Jr. to P. Hoffmann, letter dated April 15, 1929. Fagus archives, file 185. Only numbers 8 (main entrance), 22 (stack of rough lasts) and 54 (portrait of Benscheidt Sr.) are selected for publication. *Cf.* Hoffmann 1930.

23 Fagus factory to *Schuhfabrikanten-Zeitung*, letter dated October 4, 1929. Fagus archives, file 185. Benscheidt Jr. exchanged his portrait picture (number 51) at the last minute for a picture from another photographer because it "didn't resemble him." *Cf.* Benscheidt Sr. in a letter to *Schuhfabrikanten-Zeitung*, December 13, 1929.

24 *Cf.* Renger-Patzsch 1960, p. 550. Gropius and Meyer were most certainly not involved in commissioning the Fagus series. They had no contact with Renger-Patzsch; the architecture photographs were mailed to them from the Fagus factory.

25 Exhibition catalog 1931, no page number.

1 No documents pertaining to the tombstone survive in the Fagus archives. Members of the Benscheidt family have confirmed, however, that Gropius and Meyer created the design.

2 We can infer the time of this renovation work from the date of the two photographs taken of the completed kitchen in the first half of 1923.

3 Almost all the furnishings from Benscheidt Jr.'s house were auctioned off in 1987. *Cf.* Sotheby's auction catalog for 1987.

4 "2 rooms Alfeld" are mentioned in the monthly report of the Bauhaus mural workshop for December 1923. HStA Weimar, Bauhaus documents, file 177, sheet 13.

5 Cabinetmaker Georg Lautenbauch must not be mistaken for Wroclaw architect Heinrich Lauterbach; he was also never a member of the Bauhaus. *Cf.* 1922 Dessau address directory, p. 222.

6 *Cf.* Jaeggi 1994, obj. No. 165e, p. 403, where the pieces are erroneously counted among the office furnishings of the Fagus factory.

7 W. Gropius to C. Benscheidt Sr., letter dated March 3, 1924. Fagus archives, file 30.

8 W. Gropius to C. Benscheidt Sr., letter dated October 19, 1925 (invoice). Fagus archives, file 31.

9 Benscheidt Sr. ordered the lamp after seeing photographs in Alfeld. *Cf.* Gropius (office correspondence) to C. Benscheidt Sr., letter dated May 30, 1924. Fagus archives, file 30.

10 According to account books at Gropius's office, 1924–1928. BHA.

11 The team members at the practice marked all plans and draft documents with a monogram or with initials. This identified them as having worked on the plan or having drawn it. It did not identify them as the designer. The full signature *Fieger* therefore supports the theory that he was the designer. Fieger's estate is stored at the Bauhaus in Dessau.

12 W. Gropius to C. Benscheidt Sr., letter dated October 28, 1925. Fagus archives, file 31.

13 Gropius wanted to use the same bright yellow bricks from C. Benscheidt Sr.'s son-in-law for the employment ministry building in Dessau. *Cf.* Gropius (office correspondence) to C. Benscheidt Sr., letter dated February 27, 1928. Fagus archives, file 33.

14 At the beginning of July 1928, Neufert produced additional plans for renovating the Lange house, located on the property adjoining the Fagus factory and also owned by Benscheidt. Three ground plans still exist in the Fagus archives.

Bibliography

Anonymous: "Eine Heimstätte deutscher Industrie." In *Der Schuhmarkt* 1899, No. 13 (March 31), pp. 45–54.

Anonymous: "Das Fagus-Werk Karl Benscheidt, Alfeld." In *Niedersächsische Zeitschrift für Industrie und Gewerbe* 22. 1928, No. 12 (March 21), pp. 92–94.

Anonymous (K.G.): "50 Jahre Fagus-Werk Karl Benscheidt in Alfeld." In *Alfelder Zeitung* April 7, 1961.

Anonymous: "Gropius-Design 1924–1926. Schlichte deutsche Küchenmöbel in Monte Carlo." In *Antiquitäten-Zeitung* 1987, No. 8, p. 195.

Angulus Varus Gesellschaft (eds.): *Die Lösung der Fußbekleidungsfrage in der Praxis.* no date [probably 1928].

Banham, Reyner: *Theory and Design in the First Machine Age.* London 1960.

Banham, Reyner: *A Concrete Atlantis. US Industrial Building and European Modern Architecture.* Cambridge, Mass. 1986.

Barner, Wilhelm: "Carl Benscheidt d. Ä., 1858–1947." Special edition from: *Niedersächsische Lebensbilder* 3. 1957, pp. 1–12.

Bauverein Alfeld (eds.): *Vierzig Jahre Gemeinnütziger Bauverien für den Kreis Alfeld e. G.m.b.H. 1899–1939.* Alfeld Leine 1940.

Behne, Adolf: "Romantiker, Pathetiker und Logiker im modernen Industriebau." In *Preußische Jahrbücher* 1913, Vol. 154 (October–December), pp. 171–174.

Behne, Adolf: "Heutige Industriebauten." In *Velhagen & Klasings Monatshefte* 28. 1913–1914, Vol. 2, No. 5 (January 1914), pp. 53–64.

Behne, Adolf: "Heutige Industriebauten." In *Die Welt des Kaufmanns* October 1914, No. 11 (June), pp. 215–219.

Behne, Adolf: "Fabrikbau als Reklame." In *Das Plakat* November 1920, No. 6, pp. 274–276.

Behne, Adolf: "Neue Kräfte in userer Architektur." In *Feuer* 3. 1922, No. 8 (May), pp. 269–276.

Behne, Adolf: "Entwürfe und Bauten von Walter Gropius." In *Zentralblatt der Bauverwaltung* 42. 1922, No. 104 (December 24), pp. 637–640.

Behne, Adolf: "Die moderne Fabrik." In *Illustrierte Zeitung,* February 17, 1924.

Behne, Adolf: *Der moderne Zweckbau.* Munich/Vienna/Berlin 1926.

Behnsen, Jörg: "Der Fall: Das Fagus-Werk in Alfeld." In *Der Baumeister* 82. 1985, issue 10, pp. 28–31 and p. 68.

Behnsen, Jörg, and Dieter Rentschler-Weissmann: "Zur Restaurierung des Fagus-Werkes in Alfeld (Leine)." In *Berichte zur Denkmalpflege in Niedersachsen* 6. 1986, No. 1, pp. 2–11.

Behrendt, Walter Curt: "Das Pathos des Monumentalen." In *Deutsche Kunst und Dekoration* 34. 1914, pp. 219–221.

Behrendt, Walter Curt: *Der Sieg des neuen Baustils.* Stuttgart 1927.

Behrens, Peter: "Kunst und Technik." In *Berliner Tageblatt* January 25, 1909, weekend supplement "Der Zeitgeist."

Behrens, Peter: "Die Turbinenhalle der Allgemeinen Elektricitätsgesellschaft zu Berlin." In *Mitteilungen des Rheinischen Vereins für Denkmalpflege und Heimatschutz* 4. 1910, No. 1 (March 1) pp. 26–29.

Benscheidt, Carl: "Aus meinem Leben." unpublished manuscript, 1947 (private collection).

Benscheidt, Carl: "Die Herstellung von Schuhleisten in Deutschland." In *Holz als Roh- und Werkstoff* 9.1951, pp. 342–348.

Benscheidt, Karl: "Die moderne Schuhleistenfabrikation." In *Die Berufsschulklasse für Schuhmacher und Sattler* 2. 1927, No. 10 (October 15), pp. 289–303.

Benscheidt, Karl: *Der gesunde Fuß und sein Leben.* Alfeld 1957.

Beutinger, Emil: "Die Faguswerke in Alfeld a. L." In *Der Industriebau* 4. 1913, No. 1 (January 15), pp. 11–19.

Bosse: "Alfeld. Perle des Leinetales." In *Sonderbeilage zum Hanoverschen Kurier* January 23,1930.

Brown, William J.: "Walter Gropius and Grain Elevators. Misreading Photographs." In *History of Photography* 17.1993, No. 3, pp. 304–308.

Brüning, Ute: "Die Druck- und Reklamewerkstatt: Von Typographie zur Werbung." In Exhibition catalog 1988, pp. 154–197.

Buddensieg, Tilmann, and Henning Rogge: *Industriekutlur. Peter Behrens und die AEG 1907–1914.* Berlin 1979.

Cohen, Jean-Louis: *Scenes of the World to Come. European Architecture and the American Challenge 1893–1960.* Paris 1995.

Croyle, C. Arthur: " The Calligraphy of Max Hertwig." In: *Calligraphy Review* 6. 1988, No. 1, pp. 40–47.

Dieling, Otto: *25 Jahre Fagus-Werk, Karl Benscheidt, Alfeld-Leine.* Alfeldie 1936.

Exhibition catalog 1931: *Walter Gropius.* Ständige Bauwelt-Musterschau Berlin. Berlin 1930.

Exhibition catalog 1930: *Walter Gropius.* Kestner-Gesellschaft, Hanover (with an introduction by Justus Bier). Hanover 1931.

Exhibition catalog 1982: *Herbert Bayer. Das künstlerische Werk 1918–1938.* Bauhaus Archiv Berlin, and Gewerbemuseum Basel. Berlin 1982.

Exhibition catalog 1988: *Experiment Bauhaus.* Bauhaus Dessau (edited by Baushaus archives, Berlin). Berlin 1988.

Exhibition catalog 1990: *"Typographie kann unter Umständen Kunst sein." Vordemberge-Gildewart. Typographie und Werbegestalung.* Wiesbaden/Hanover/Zurich 1990.

Exhibition catalog 1993–1994: *Moderne Baukunst 1900–1914. Die Photosammlung des Deutschen Museums für Kunst in Handel und Gewerbe.* Kaiser Wilhelm Museum Krefeld and Karl Ernst Osthaus-Museum Hagen. Oberhausen 1993.

Exhibition catalog 1995–1996: *Das A und O des Bauhauses.* Bauhaus Archiv Berlin, Württembergischer Kunstverein Stuttgart and Gerhard-Marcks-Haus Bremen. Leipzig 1995.

Exhibition catalog 1997: *Albert Renger-Patzsch.* Museum Folkwang Essen. Krefeld 1997.

Exhibition catalog 1997–1998: *Albert Renger-Patzsch. Meisterwerke.* Sprengel Museum Hanover, Württembergischer Kunstverein Stuttgart, Foto-Museum Winterthur and Haus der Kunst, Munich. Munich/Paris/London 1997.

Exhibition catalog 1997–1998: *Deutsches Museum für Kunst in Handel und Gewerbe 1909–1919.* Kaiser Wilhelm Museum Krefeld and Karl Ernst Osthaus-Museum Hagen. Gent/Antwerp 1997.

Franz, W.: *Fabrikbauten.* (Handbuch der Architektur, Vol. 4.2.5.) Leipzig 1923.

Giedion, Sigfried. "Walter Gropius et l'architecture en Allemagne." In *Cahiers d'art* 1930, No.2, pp. 95–103.

Giedion, Sigfried: "Walter Gropius und die Architektur in Deutschland." In *Neue Zürcher Zeitung* May 3 and 4, 1930.

Giedion, Sigfried: *Walter Gropius.* Paris 1931.

Giedion, Sigfried: *Space, Time and Architecture.* Cambridge, Mass., 1941.

Giedion, Sigfried: *Walter Gropius. Mensch und Werk.* Stuttgart 1954 (English edition: New York 1954.

Giedion, Sigfried: *Die Herrschaft der Mechanisierung.* Frankfurt/Main 1982 (original English edition: New York 1948).

Gordon, B.F.: "The Fagus Factory." In *Architectural Record* 169. 1981, No. 7, pp. 114–117.

Grimshaw, Robert: *Die kaufmännische Propaganda und Reklame vom wissenschaftlichen, organisatorischen, künstlerschen und praktischen Standpunkt aus betrachtet.* Dresden 1913.

Grönwald, Bernd: "Faguswerk und Bauhaus." In *form + zweck* 18.1986, No. 6, pp. 10–15.

Gropius, Walter: "†ber das Wesen des verschiedenen Kunstwollens im Orient und Occident." 1910 (unpublished). Manuscript in Bauhaus Archiv Berlin.

Gropius, Walter: "Monumentale Kunst und Industriebau." Lecture, presented on April 10,1911, in the Folkwang Museum at Hagen. Printed in: Probst, Hartmut, and Christian Schädlich (eds.): *Walter Gropius* Vol.3 (Berlin 1988), pp. 28–51.

Gropius, Walter: "Sind beim Bau von Industriegebäuden künstlerische Gesichtspunkte mit praktischen und wirtschaftlichen vereinbar?" In *Der Kaufmann und das Leben* 1911, No.12 (December), pp. 189–191. Reprinted in *Der Industriebau* 3.1912, No. 1 (January 15), pp. 5ff.

Gropius, Walter: "Faltblatt zur Wanderausstellung 18 des Deutschen Museums für Kunst in Handel und Gewerbe, 1911." In *Der Industriebau* 3.1912, No. 2 (February 15), p. 46.

Gropius, Walter: "Die Entwicklung moderner Industriebaukunst." In *Jahrbuch des Deutschen Werkbundes* 2. 1913, pp. 17–22.

Gropius, Walter: "Der stilbildende Wert industrieller Bauformen." In *Jahrbuch des Deutschen Werkbundes* 3. 1914, pp. 29–32.

Gropius, Walter: *Internationale Architektur.* Munich 1925 (2nd edition 1927).

Gropius, Walter: "glasbau." In *Die Bauzeitung* 23. 1926, No. 20 (May 25), pp. 159–162.

Gropius, Walter: "Stellungnahme zum Artikel 'Neue Fabrikbauten in Alfeld (Leine).'" In *Deutsche Bauzeitung* 62. 1928, No. 66 (August 18), p. 568.

Gropius, Walter: *Architektur. Wege zu einer optischen Kultur.* Frankfurt on Main/Hamburg 1956 (2nd edition Frankfurt on Main 1982; original English edition New York 1955).

Gropius, Walter: "Curtain Wall Progression in the Work of Walter Gropius (Architectural Details, Part 5)." In *Architectural Record* 137. 1965, February issue, pp. 133–139.

Gropius, Walter, and Adolf Meyer (eds.): *Walter Gropius mit Adolf Meyer, Weimar. Bauten.* Berlin, no date [1923].

Heckert, Virginia: "'Lernt die Welt sehen.' Zu den pädagogischen Aspekten der Arbeiten Albert Renger-Patzschs und der Fotografie der Neuen Sachlichkeit." In *Ausstellungskatalog 1997*, pp. 6–21.

Hegemann, Werner: *Reihenhaus-Fassaden. Geschäfts- und Wohnhäuser aus alter und neuer Zeit.* Berlin 1929.

Heise, Georg: *Die Welt ist schön. 100 photographische Aufnahmen von Albert Renger-Patzsch.* Munich 1928.

Hesse-Frielinghaus, Herta (and others): *Karl Ernst Osthaus. Leben und Werk.* Recklinghausen 1971.

Hesse-Wartegg, Ernst von: *Amerika als neueste Weltmacht der Industrie.* Stuttgart/Berlin/Leipzig, no date [1908].

Hitchcock, Henry-Russell: *Modern Architecture. Romanticism and Reintegration.* New York 1929 (Reprint: New York 1970).

Hitchcock, Henry-Russell: *Architecture Nineteenth and Twentieth Centuries.* Harmondsworth 1958.

Hoeber, Fritz: *Peter Behrens.* Munich 1913.

Hoffmann, Paul: "Neue Fabrikbauten in Alfeld (Leine)." In *Deutsche Bauzeitung* 62. 1928, No. 51 (June 27), pp. 436–439.

Hoffmann, Paul: "Ein Besuch in den Fagus-Werken Carl Benscheidt." In *Schuhfabrikanten Zeitung* 11. 1930, No. 3 (January 8), pp. 9–16.

Holitscher, Arthur: *Amerika. Heute und morgen.* Berlin 1912.

Isaacs, Reginald R.: *Walter Gropius. Der Mensch und sein Werk.* Vol. I, Berlin 1983 (abridged English edition Boston 1991).

Jaeger, Roland: "Johannes Molzahn (1892–1956) als Gebrauchsgraphiker und Buchgestalter." In *Börsenblatt für den Deutschen Buchhandel* 1992, No. 52, pp. A225–A234.

Jaeggi, Annemarie: *Adolf Meyer. Der zweite Mann. Ein Architekt im Schatten von Walter Gropius.* Berlin 1994.

Jaeggi, Annemarie: "Die plastische Kraft des Wortes: Entwerfen im Gespräch. Zur Arbeitsmethode von Walter Gropius" In *Archithese* 25. 1995, No. 4, pp. 8–13.